IMAGES
of America

LACONIA MOTORCYCLE WEEK

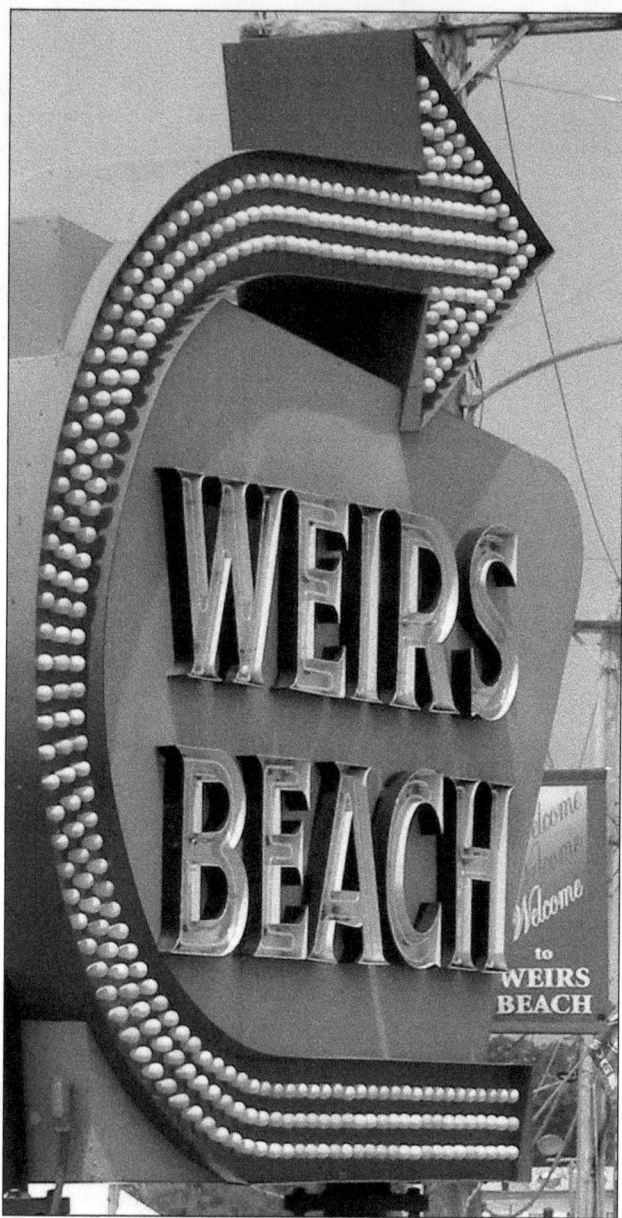

The Weirs Beach sign at the junction of U.S. Route 3 and Lakeside Avenue has greeted visitors to Weirs Beach since 1956. In 2002, with the help of Alison Hildebrand, the Weirs Action Committee, and the city of Laconia, the sign was refurbished in its original art deco style. For many motorcyclists, the sign is a major symbol of Laconia Motorcycle Week. The flashing arrow on the sign points down Lakeside Avenue, which to many people is the main street during motorcycle week. Many other landmarks from the time between 1916 and 1998 have been changed forever but this sign has remained a constant. (Courtesy of W. Stephen Loughlin.)

On the cover: Riders line up for instructions before the start of racing at Belknap Recreation Area. The riders who will be in the race pay close attention to directions because any mistake could cost them the race. (Courtesy of Butch Baer.)

IMAGES
of America

LACONIA MOTORCYCLE WEEK

Charlie St. Clair and Jennifer Anderson

ARCADIA
PUBLISHING

Published by Arcadia Publishing
Charleston, South Carolina

Library of Congress Catalog Card Number: 2007925450

For all general information contact Arcadia Publishing at:
Telephone 843-853-2070
Fax 843-853-0044
E-mail sales@arcadiapublishing.com
For customer service and orders:
Toll-Free 1-888-313-2665

Visit us on the Internet at www.arcadiapublishing.com

*This book is dedicated to all of the motorcycle enthusiasts
around the world who have supported Laconia Motorcycle Week.
Thanks to you, Laconia Motorcycle Week continues to thrive!*

CONTENTS

ACKNOWLEDGMENTS

Since the early years of Laconia Motorcycle Week, hundreds of motorcycle enthusiasts have contributed their valuable time towards sustaining the nation's oldest rally. It is impossible to thank all of those volunteers individually but they have helped ensure through their dedication and shared passion of motorcycling that future enthusiasts will enjoy Laconia Motorcycle Week.

Many people and organizations came together in a united effort to help make this book possible. We would like to specifically thank the Baer family, including Butch, Tom, Brenda, and Jim. We would also like to thank Jenna Carroll-Plante with the Laconia Historical Society, Raymond Reed, Bob Coy, Warren Huse, Gordon King, Pam Paquette, and Peter Karagianis for their extensive knowledge of Laconia's history.

Finally, thank you to Arcadia Publishing for reaching out to us years ago and encouraging this project. If not for their diligence and creativity, we may not have been able to accomplish this book. A special thank you to our editor, Erin Rocha, for her undaunted willingness to help us and for answering our endless questions.

INTRODUCTION

The sport of motorcycling had its early beginnings at the dawn of the 20th century. With each year and each new model of motorcycle, the popularity grew, and enthusiasts began touring to enjoy the scenic vistas around them. The state of New Hampshire enjoyed visitors from those early periods as motorcyclists toured around the various regions to see the sights of the lakes and mountains. In 1916, a modest crowd of 100 to 150 motorcyclists rode to Laconia for the first gypsy tour, which was organized by motorcycle shops and dealers in central and southern New England. These motorcyclists spent several days in the area taking advantage of the amenities. Thus Laconia Motorcycle Week began, and these folks made Laconia a yearly destination when the weather became warm. Motorcyclists spent several days to a week in the Laconia-Weirs Beach area, and their stays were extended because during this time period, travel, especially on a motorcycle, was long, and enthusiasts enjoyed the restful break in Laconia from their trip.

The Federation of American Motorcycles (FAM) was the first group to sanction these tours in 1917, and then after it disbanded in 1919, the Motorcycle and Allied Trades Association (M&ATA) took over the sanction until the American Motorcycle Association (AMA) was formed in 1924. The term gypsy tour refers to an organized tour with a set destination. It did not take long for Laconia Motorcycle Week to evolve and include motorcycle-related events and racing. The unorganized motorcycle hill climbs were held on Tower Street off of Lakeside Avenue, while other races took place anywhere they could be managed.

The gypsy tour continued through the 1920s and the 1930s. In 1938, a motorcycle enthusiast named Fritzie Baer was instrumental in bringing the road races to Belknap Recreation Area (now Gunstock Mountain Resort) with the help of the New England Motorcycle Dealers Association. For more than 30 years, Baer worked hard at keeping the Laconia motorcycle rally at full steam. He and his supporters, the Red Hat Brigades, held affections from motorcyclists from around the country.

The 1960s were a time of upheaval around the country. In 1960, the name gypsy tour was no longer used by the AMA and the weeklong rally was referred to only as motorcycle week or Laconia. In 1962, the last hill climbs were held at Belknap Recreation Area and would not return for many years. In 1964, the races were moved to the track in Loudon 15 miles south of Laconia and were named the Laconia Classic.

At Weirs Beach, relations between the visiting motorcyclists and the local police chief were strained and many motorcyclists were told not to come back because they were no longer welcome. In 1965, a law was passed by the state of New Hampshire that people in groups larger than three had to be mobile or they could be arrested. The law was passed before the start of motorcycle week that year. Trouble did break out between some motorcyclists, police, locals, and the national guard, which has since became known as the "riot of '65." There are many stories about what took place in 1965. Some reports had thousands of people joined in a full-scale riot that claimed half of Weirs Beach by fire. The most accurate reporting has come from a series of news stories, personal interviews, and photographs taken that night. Some of these reports suggest that what happened bordered on a police riot.

As a result of the riot of 1965, all events in Laconia were cancelled except for the races in Loudon. Laconia Motorcycle Week became motorcycle weekend. By 1984, the Laconia Classic was renamed the Loudon Classic.

The 1970s and 1980s had high and low points for the sport of motorcycling and for Laconia Motorcycle Week. The purchases of motorcycles slowed during these times and the attendance to area rallies also dropped. In 1975, all camping along New Hampshire State Route 106 was outlawed and the number of visiting motorcyclists dropped to 25,000–30,000 in the years following. Throughout the 1980s, Laconia Motorcycle Weekend stayed about the same size in numbers, but the other two national rallies at Sturgis and Daytona were growing in size and popularity. In 1990 on the 50th anniversary of the Sturgis rally in South Dakota, over 400,000 motorcyclists attended the weeklong event. The *Boston Sunday Globe* did a story on the rally in Sturgis that year and compared it to Laconia's rally and history. Local businesses and organizations such as Funspot, Meredith Harley-Davidson, and the Lakeside Sharks motorcycle club got together and, with help from the AMA, worked towards bringing back motorcycle week as it was before 1965.

With the help of various individuals and businesses, the Laconia Motorcycle Week association was formed, and in 1991, the rally was once again called Laconia Motorcycle Week with a rally headquarters set up in Weirs Beach and motorcycle events added to fill up the week. The association was formed as a not-for-profit organization with a board of directors, an executive director, and later a director. The association's year-long mission is to promote Laconia Motorcycle Week and the state of New Hampshire as a place for motorcycle enthusiasts to visit. In 1992, the AMA resumed using the term gypsy tour and Laconia Motorcycle Week was officially re-sanctioned. The hill climbs returned to Gunstock Mountain Resort in 1993, and the attendance to the rally continued to rise.

The 75th anniversary in 1998 saw a record-breaking attendance with over 300,000 motorcyclists coming to the state of New Hampshire for Laconia Motorcycle Week. The rally has averaged over 375,000 people since 1998, and 2008 will celebrate the 85th anniversary of the oldest national motorcycle rally in the United States.

Laconia Motorcycle Week is now made up of hundreds of events around the state of New Hampshire. Enthusiasts can enjoy vintage, road, flat track, and sidecar racing from Laconia to Loudon to Rochester. The hill climb at Gunstock Mountain Resort now averages well over 7,000 people for its one-day event. In the White Mountain region, enthusiasts can enjoy two days of motorcycle-only traffic up the Mount Washington Auto Road and see the sights from the highest elevation in the northeast. More events are added every year to ensure that visitors from around the world can enjoy and take part in everything motorcycle related.

This book would not have been possible without the help from many individuals and organizations that were willing to share their expertise, knowledge, and photographs. As the oldest national rally in the country, Laconia Motorcycle Week can be experienced and treasured for generations to come with the help of this book. There are undoubtedly many more sources of photographs and information than are seen here; the task of finding them shall be left to future motorcycle-week enthusiasts. It is hoped that residents of the state of New Hampshire and motorcycle enthusiasts from around the world will gain a new appreciation for the gem that is Laconia Motorcycle Week. With its rich history and promising future, it is surely a rally that will live on.

One

THE GYPSY TOUR YEARS

Weirs Beach and Laconia have been a destination for vacationers since the mid-1800s due to the proximity to Lake Winnipesaukee. When a group of motorcycle dealers in central and southern New England decided in 1916 to organize a motorcycle tour, Laconia was decided on for the destination. That was the start of an 85-year-long relationship between the gypsy tour and the city of Laconia that continues today.

The Federation of American Motorcycles (FAM) was the first group to sanction these tours in 1917, and then after it disbanded in 1919, the Motorcycle and Allied Trades Association (M&ATA) took over the sanction until the American Motorcycle Association (AMA) was formed in 1924. The gypsy tour was sanctioned from the AMA from that point on, and it was organized by the New England Motorcycle Dealers Association. The length of the gypsy tour at Laconia has varied over the years. The first year, the tour was about four or five days long. By the 1950s, it was eight days long. From 1966 to 1990, the tour was three days long, and in 1991, it was back to nine days in length. The New England gypsy tour was sponsored by the New England Motorcycle Dealers Association and was moved to Laconia in 1938 along with the National Championship Road Races, which were also sanctioned by the AMA.

The gypsy tour was not only an organized ride but also consisted of many contests that were held for the visiting motorcyclists. The AMA-sanctioned gypsy tour is the longest-running motorcycle event in the United States.

This photograph may be one of the only known pictures of the first gypsy tour that came to Laconia and Weirs Beach in 1916. This photograph is of Lakeside Avenue taken from the boardwalk just north of the Boston and Maine Railroad station. The surface and layout of the roads during this time period meant that people could spend an entire day for a 100-mile trip. Most of the riders were from Massachusetts. It is believed that up to 150 motorcycles and riders made the trip. The gypsy tour was organized by motorcycle shops in southern New England. (Courtesy of Raymond Reed.)

This group from the Bay State Motorcycle Club of Massachusetts arrived for the gypsy tour at Weirs Beach in 1918. Local reports estimated that 300 motorcycles arrived for the tour, but it is unclear if all were members of the motorcycle club. The street on which the motorcycles are parked is Lakeside Avenue. The photograph is looking north. In the center top of the photograph is where the Weirs Beach General Store is today. Lake Winnipesaukee is on the right-hand side. This street was not paved at the time. Most of the riders and their passengers were wearing their Sunday best clothes. (Courtesy of Warren Huse.)

This motorcyclist poses on his Indian motorcycle in 1920 on Lakeside Avenue at Weirs Beach. This is the fifth year of the gypsy tour at Laconia now sponsored by the M&ATA. In the background is the Boston and Maine Railroad station located on what is today the Weirs Beach boardwalk. (Courtesy of Ann Lamere.)

In this 1920 photograph, Lee Lamere is seen standing behind his friend, Blossom Cox. They are standing on New Salem Street in Laconia, which is to the rear of the Boston and Maine Railroad station in downtown. Lamere's Indian motorcycle is also in the photograph. Lamere's motorcycle shop sold and serviced Indian motorcycles on the south side of Laconia. (Courtesy of Ann Lamere.)

This photograph is from Lakeside Avenue in Weirs Beach. It looks like most of the riders got to their motorcycles in time for the picture to be taken. This photograph is from the gypsy tour in 1919, and Lakeside Avenue was and is considered to be the main street of the tour. Before national racing came in 1938, Lakeside Avenue was the main destination for the riders. (Courtesy of Raymond Reed.)

This postcard photograph is of the M&ATA-sanctioned gypsy tour in Laconia in 1923. The correspondence on the back of the card stated that 800 motorcycles were in town and over 1,000 riders and passengers. The next year, the AMA took over the M&ATA and became the sanctioning group for the gypsy tour. (Courtesy of Wayne L. Caveney.)

This photograph from 1920 was taken on Main Street in Laconia. Pictured second from the right in the front is Lee Lamere. He is stopped on the road with his friends, including Blossom Cox, who is directly behind him. Lamere and his friends are getting ready to ride to the Weirs for the gypsy tour. Lamere owned a motorcycle shop on Wakefield Court. (Courtesy of Ann Lamere.)

In the early 1930s, Main Street in Laconia was becoming a gathering place for riders in town for the gypsy tour. There were plenty of shops and places to grab a meal. It is less than six miles to Weirs Beach from Main Street in Laconia and less than 12 miles to Belknap Recreation Area. Many of the store owners had special sales for the riders. (Courtesy of Raymond Reed.)

Here a group of riders in 1938 or 1939 are taking a right turn onto Canal Street in downtown Laconia. The lack of people standing to watch would dispel the notion of this being part of an organized parade. Parades are one of the most famous past times of gypsy tours. (Courtesy of Laconia Historical Society.)

In this photograph, a parade is making its way along Main Street in Laconia in the late 1930s. This may be the parade to Belknap Recreation Area, or it may just be a tour taking riders during the rally to other parts of town. It was not unusual then nor is it now to see a group of 50 or more motorcyclists riding together. (Courtesy of Laconia Historical Society.)

This group of riders has taken up a large part of Main Street as they ride through Laconia. Unlike today, Main Street in downtown was a two-way road in the 1930s. None of the motorcyclists have any gear packed on their bikes, which is another indication that this is just a ride around town and that the riders are already checked into rooms or cabins somewhere. (Courtesy of Laconia Historical Society.)

These motorcycles are parked on Main Street in Laconia. The second motorcycle in from the front has the name "Willie" printed on the bag, while the first one has what appears to be sheep skin on the seat for comfort. Most of the motorcycles at this time had a running light on the top of the front fender. (Courtesy of John Mont and Joan Mont Shaw.)

Main Street in downtown Laconia is filling up with motorcycles in this 1939 shot. Since there are not many riders standing around, they may be visiting different shops around town. Ray's Diner is at the end of the street on the left at the junction of Church Street and Main Street. (Courtesy of John Mont and Joan Mont Shaw.)

In June of 1939 Dot Robinson and her daughter Betty Jane stopped by the Baer homestead in Springfield, Massachusetts, while on their way to Laconia. Dot is seen here wearing her Motor Maids uniform, of which she was the president. She rode from Detroit, Michigan, to attend the gypsy tour and races at Laconia and was well known by many at the gypsy tour. (Courtesy of Butch Baer.)

The motorcyclists are heading north towards the Weirs in this photograph from the late 1940s. They are in Normandin Square, which is now known as Busy Corner. The two closest motorcycles are from New York. From the looks of all of the gear, they may have been on their way to Belknap Recreation Area to camp. (Courtesy of Raymond Reed.)

Dot Robinson (driving the motorcycle) and her daughter Betty Jane (in the sidecar) are outside the main entrance to Belknap Recreation Area in 1941. Note the chrome front end of the sidecar. The road that they are traveling on is State Route 11A and the sidecar seems to take up most of the road. The Arlberg Inn, seen to the right side of the photograph, was a favorite place to stay for many motorcyclists. (Courtesy of Butch Baer.)

Robinson (right) and two other Motor Maids are doing an interview on WLNH, the local AM radio station. On the table in front of Robinson is her camera. WLNH played a big part in the gypsy tour and then the races. Most events had live coverage, with many of the downtown stores having the station playing during their hours of operation. (Courtesy of Butch Baer.)

This photograph is of an auxiliary group of the Fritzie's Roamers. The roamers were a motorcycle club out of the Springfield, Massachusetts, area where Fritzie Baer was originally from. This photograph was taken at Belknap Recreation Area in the late 1940s. It was not common for most clubs to have an auxiliary group. Note how the boots shine even in a picture. Like most clubs of the time, much care was given to one's uniform. (Courtesy of Butch Baer.)

This lucky rider has parked on Church Street alongside the Laconia Library in the late 1940s. He and his motorcycle are a big draw for three local ladies. The lawn around Laconia Library became an area for social gatherings during motorcycle week. Around his waist, the rider is wearing a kidney belt for protection from rough roads and the shaking of the motorcycle. (Courtesy of Raymond Reed.)

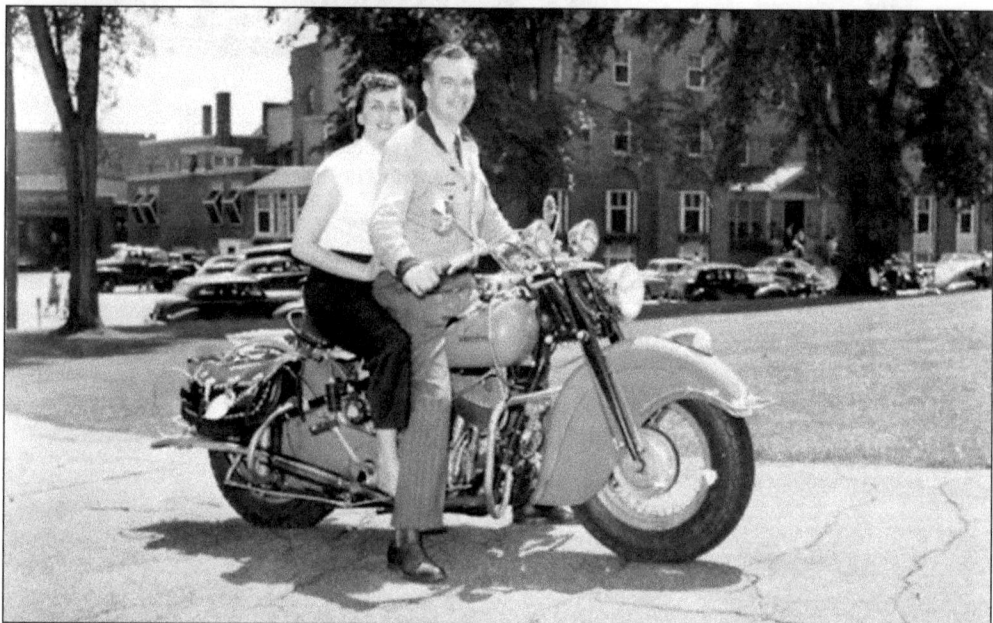

Also taking advantage of the setting of the Laconia Library is Norm Hubbard and Barbara Lyman. These two individuals were members of the Greater Laconia Weirs Beach Chamber of Commerce. Across the street from this location is the Laconia Tavern, another popular spot to get a room for the gypsy tour. This photograph was taken just before the gypsy tour in 1948. (Courtesy of Butch Baer.)

Motorcycling Digest

Official Organ of the New England Motorcycle Dealers' Association, Inc.

VOL. XIII	WEYMOUTH 89, MASSACHUSETTS	NUMBER 3

Official Program

27th Annual
New England Gypsy Tour
—•——and——•—
100-Mile National Championship Road Race

LACONIA - GILFORD, N. H.

JUNE 21, 22, 1947

This cover of the 1947 *Motorcycling Digest*, which was the official program (organ) of the New England Motorcycle Dealer's Association (as is noted on the cover), served as the official program for the gypsy tour and the 100-mile National Championship Road Race at Belknap Recreation Area. In programs such as this one, a rider saw advertisements from local businesses and others in or around New England, pictures from previous tours and races, and detailed information about what would be going on. The New England Motorcycle Dealer's Association sponsored both the gypsy tour and the national road races at Laconia for decades. On this cover, it says the 27th annual, but the races and the gypsy tour were not held during the war years from 1942 through 1945. Because of this, Laconia Motorcycle Week was no longer considered an annual rally. Today the New England Harley-Davidson Dealer's Association is the off-shoot of the original New England Motorcycle Dealers' Association. (Courtesy of the Laconia Motorcycle Week Association.)

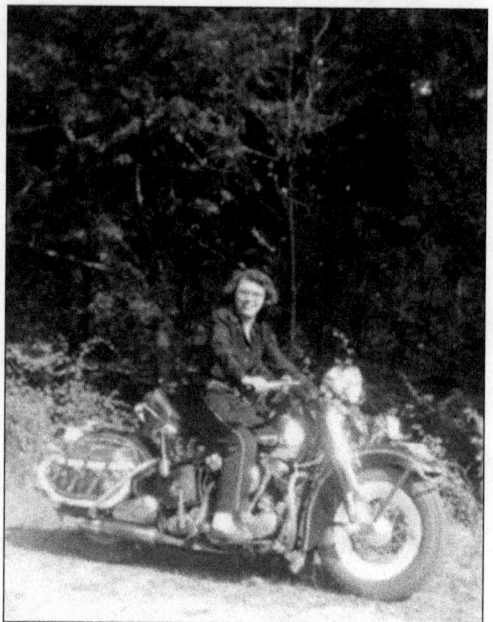

Al Chase and Lorraine Gilman Chase are seen here posing on Al's Harley-Davidson Panhead at Belknap Recreation Area during motorcycle week in 1949. They, like many riders, did not sleep very much, because they were spending as much time as possible at the Belknap Recreation Area, the Weirs, or downtown Laconia. The Chases are wearing matching riding pants, which was popular even among those riders not in motorcycle clubs. (Courtesy Lorraine Chase.)

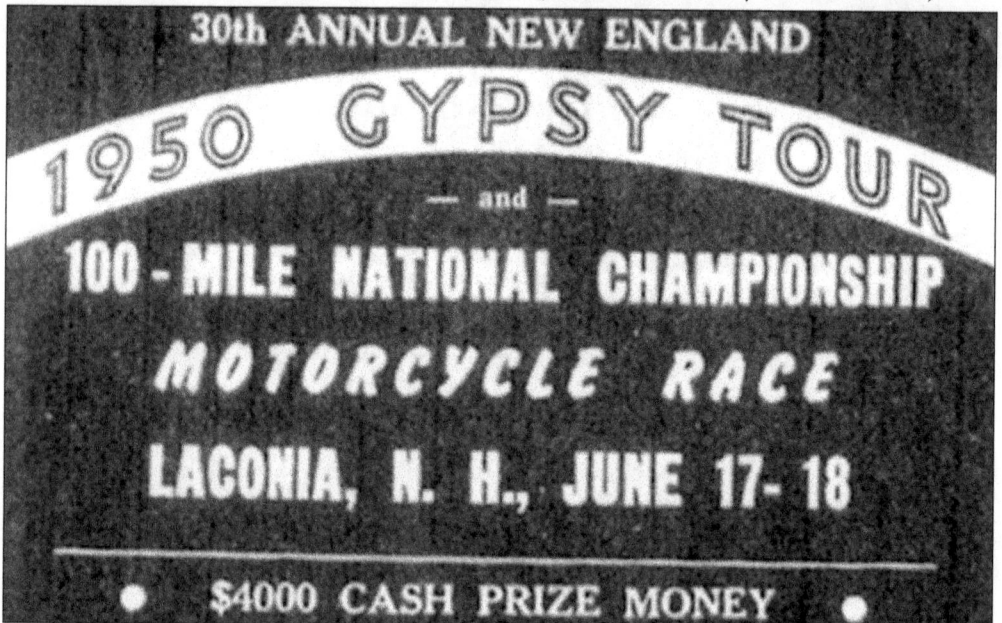

30th ANNUAL NEW ENGLAND
1950 GYPSY TOUR
— and —
100 - MILE NATIONAL CHAMPIONSHIP
MOTORCYCLE RACE
LACONIA, N. H., JUNE 17- 18

● $4000 CASH PRIZE MONEY ●

This is an advertisement for the 1950 gypsy tour and 100-Mile National Championship Road Race at Laconia. The card lists this as the 30 year of the gypsy tour because there was no gypsy tour or racing during the war from 1942 to 1945. In 1950, most, but not all events were limited to the weekend. The prize money for the winners of the races was some of the highest in the country at this time. (Courtesy of Butch Baer.)

This photograph of an Indian motorcycle dealership in Laconia which was owned and operated by Carle Johnson in the 1940s. The shop was located on Start Street, where one of Johnson's sons still lives today. During the gypsy tour, the shop was a beehive of activity. He later moved his shop to Union Avenue across from the Laconia High School. Many students who were interested in motorcycles spent much of their free time at the shop and Johnson was glad to talk motorcycles with them. (Courtesy of Bill and Sue Vachon.)

This is a display on Main Street in downtown Laconia to advertise Johnson's Indian motorcycle dealership. This photograph was taken in 1948 and Fritzie Baer is on the right with Barbara Lyman on the left. Baer was an employee of the Indian Motorcycle Company at this time and was happy to give Johnson any support he could. Having the display here may have also helped to increase business for the bookstore. (Courtesy of Butch Baer.)

This is an advertisement announcing the year's campaign for the fund-raising efforts put on by the Red Hat Brigade for the gypsy tour and the 100-Mile National Championship Road Race. The goal was to raise $3,000. The drive began during the beginning of May in most years. The Red Hat Brigade lasted until 1965. (Courtesy of Butch Baer.)

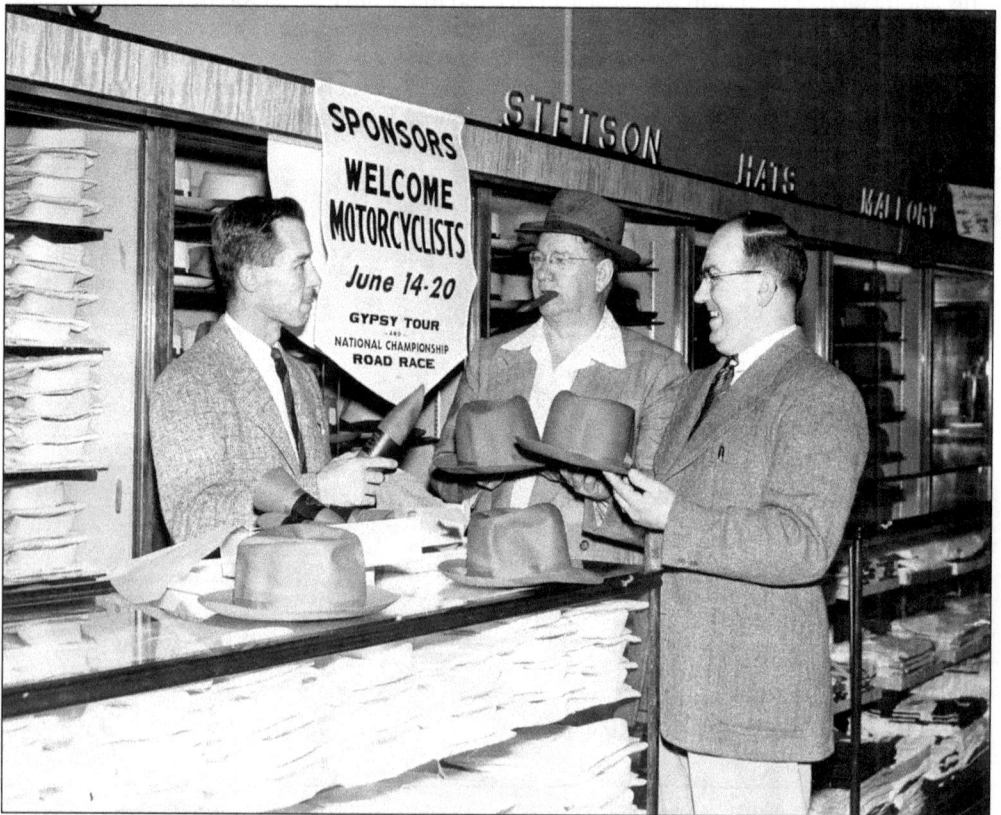

Fritzie Baer is shown here in 1954 with Peter Karagianis on his left and John O'Shea, the owner of the O'Shea's Department Store in downtown Laconia. They are in the men's hat department getting the new red hats for the Red Hat Brigade. The Red Hat Brigade helped open many doors of support from people in the area for motorcycle week. (Courtesy of Butch Baer.)

Community support for the AMA gypsy tour and the 100-Mile National Championship Road Race was spearheaded by many community leaders. They spent many hours at meetings and on site during the rally working to ensure the success of the gypsy tour and the race. From left to right are Hugh Bownes, Peter Makris, Jack Sawyer, Peter Karagianis, and Ed Hoagland. (Courtesy of Butch Baer.)

Local business owner and 1955 chairman of the Red Hat Brigade Charlie Stafford is seen here in 1955, second from the right. The poster on the wall came out months in advance of the tour and was sent out all over the nation. The poster advises to look at all motorcycle magazines and future posters for more details. (Courtesy of Butch Baer.)

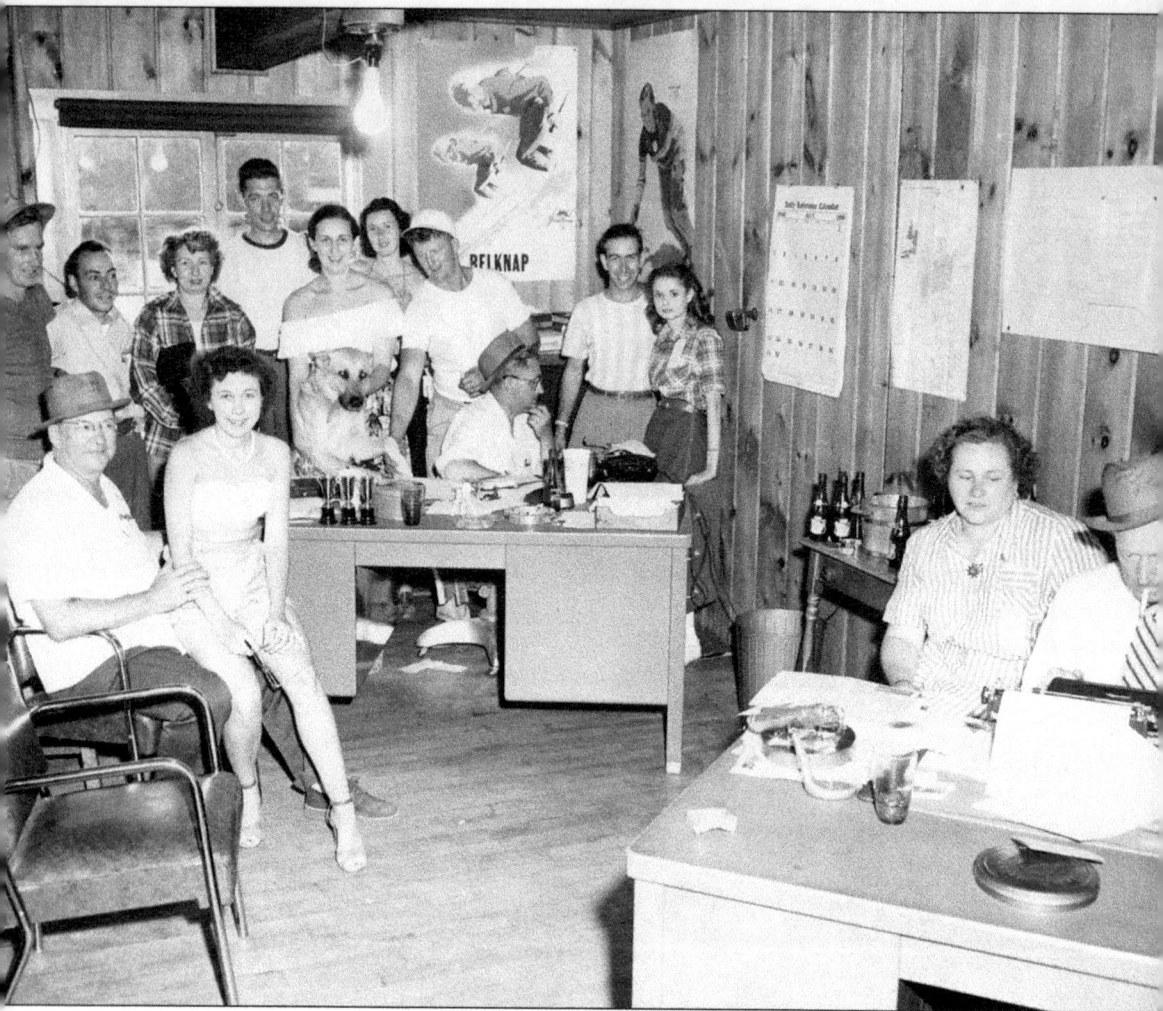

This rare photograph of a publicity meeting of some local press and staff says it all. The meeting is taking place at the Belknap Recreation Area in July 1950. Press releases were sent out all over the country at the finish of the gypsy tour and 100-Mile National Road Race with stories and results of winners. In most motorcycle magazines, August issues had large coverage of the Laconia Gypsy Tour and races. Laconia deserved and got excellent coverage in the trade magazines around the country. Fritzie Baer is sitting in the chair on the left with Barbara Hubbard, the secretary of the Laconia Chamber of Commerce, sitting on his knee. The bottles on the table on the right are Canada Dry Ginger Ale. (Courtesy of Butch Baer.)

Official Program

32nd Annual New England Gypsy Tour and 100-Mile National Championship Road Race

Belknap Recreation Area, Laconia, N. H. June 13, 14, 15, 1952

This cover of the 1952 official program of the Laconia Gypsy Tour and 100-Mile National Championship Road Races shows a great photograph of Lakeside Avenue in Weirs Beach. The dates listed on the program are June 13–15, which is when the races were held. The dates do not necessarily reflect the full dates of gypsy tour. The picture shows motorcycle clubs heading out of Weirs Beach after the best-dressed contest was held on the boardwalk. Most of the houses in the photograph remain today. However, vendors now line the lawns along the sidewalks. (Courtesy of Bob Coy.)

More and more motorcyclists are coming and going at the AMA booth. By the middle of the day, the lawn across the street at the Laconia Library will be covered with motorcyclists taking a break or even a nap. By 1950, many of the stores downtown were catering to riders with motorcycle week specials. (Courtesy of Laconia Historical Society.)

It looks like someone missed their light at the intersection of Church Street and Main Street in Laconia. With the increase of motorcycle traffic during motorcycle week, accident counts did rise although not to the degree that one would expect. Most of the roads were concrete and in very good shape. (Courtesy of Laconia Historical Society.)

This view of the Boston and Maine Railroad station shows motorcycles parked along Church Street in front of the Laconia Tavern. The library is to the right in the photograph. After 1965, most motorcycle activity in downtown Laconia was nowhere near what it was from the 1930s to 1965. (Courtesy of Laconia Historical Society.)

The Boston and Maine Railroad station in Veteran's Square was also very busy during motorcycle week. Many who did not own motorcycles took the train to both Laconia and Weirs Beach to watch the excitement. Belknap Recreation Area ran a bus from the station to the area. Several times during the gypsy tour, a bonfire was burned in the middle of Veteran's Square. This was not a sanctioned event. (Courtesy of Laconia Historical Society.)

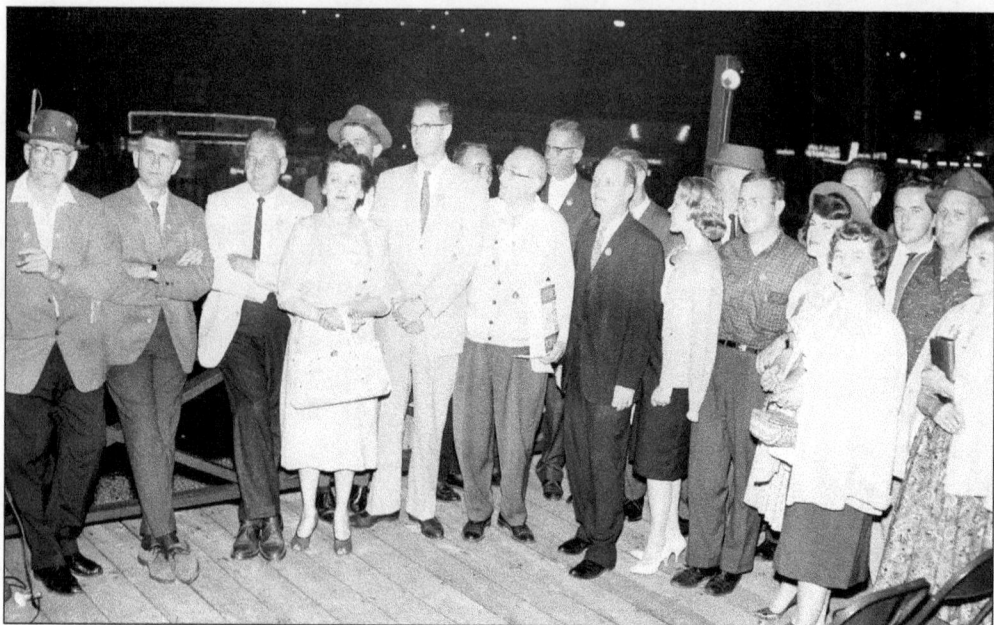

This photograph was taken on the boardwalk at Weirs Beach in the late 1950s. Fritzie Baer is wearing his red hat on the far left. Laconia mayor Ollie Huot is seventh from the left. Stewart Lamprey is fifth from the left. This is one of the many get-togethers for planning motorcycle week. (Courtesy of Butch Baer.)

Every year before the start of motorcycle week, meetings were held with the local and state public safety officers. Here Baer (fourth from left) meets with his staff, Laconia police chief Micky Dunleavy (right), and Lt. John Lockwood of the New Hampshire State Police (second from right). These press photographs showed the public how much planning went into the rally. (Courtesy of Butch Baer.)

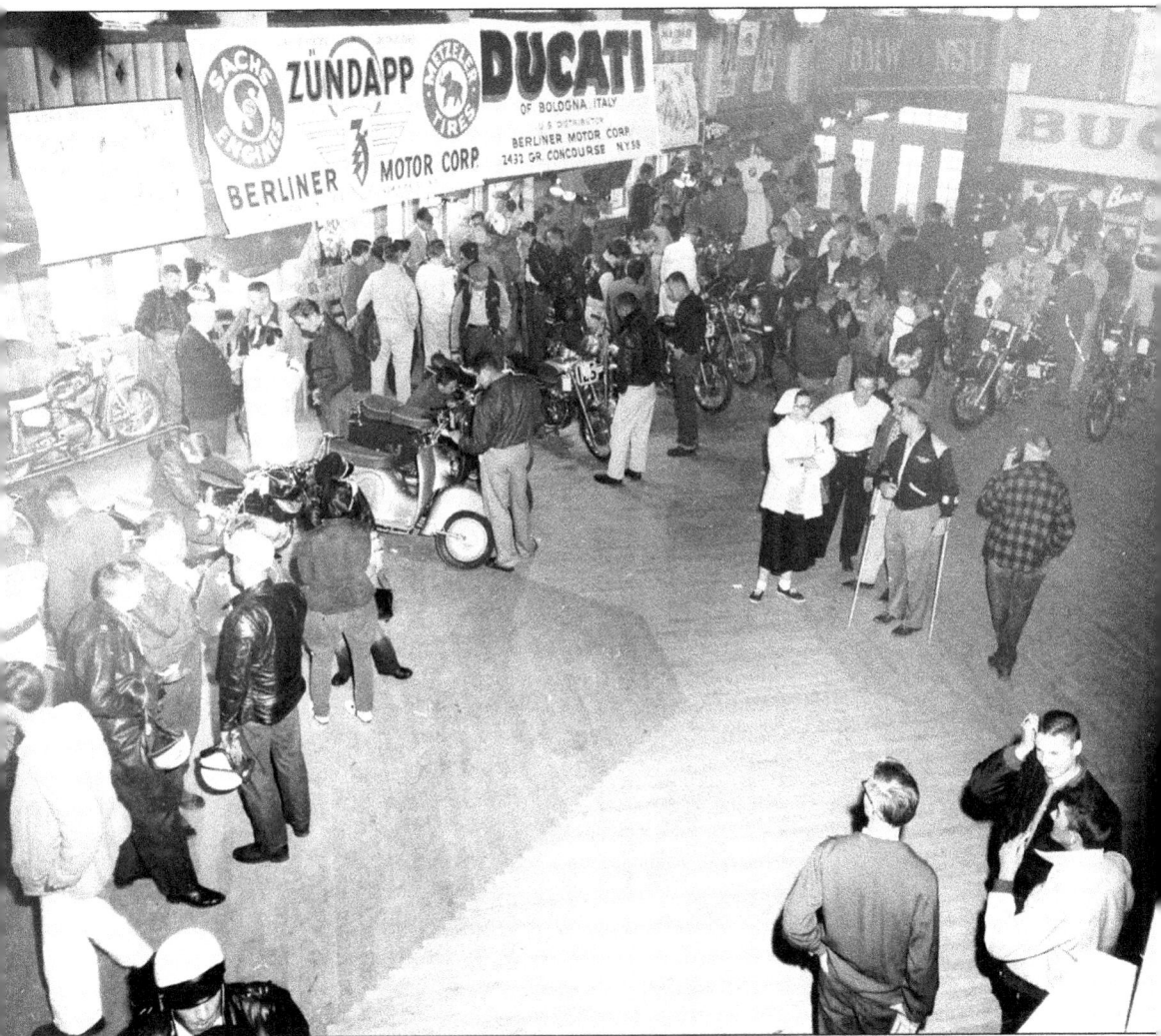

The lodge at Belknap Recreation Area was often used for motorcycle companies and motorcycle wares to set up displays. These displays were part of the gypsy tour right through 1963, the last year of the 100-Mile Championship National Road Race. The AMA officially used the term gypsy tour for the last time in 1959. From 1960 to 1991, the rally was called motorcycle week or motorcycle weekend. There was no admission cost to the display area at the lodge. (Courtesy of Butch Baer.)

The Harley-Davidson display in the lodge at the Belknap Recreation Area is visited by Fritzie Baer, wearing his red hat, and Bill Schietinger on his right. The Harley-Davidson is the Panhead model. Harley-Davidson had a large presence in Laconia and the races were often mentioned in their advertising around the country. (Courtesy of Butch Baer.)

This is the Birmingham Small Arms (BSA) display in the lodge at Belknap Recreation Area. BSA was a very popular motorcycle in the 1950s. Seen here is a BSA Gold Star club member. This 500-cubic-inch model listed for $975. Note the chrome sides on the gas tank. BSA motorcycles would win and place at many races at Laconia. (Courtesy of Butch Baer.)

Camping out at Belknap Recreation Area was a favorite pastime for thousands of campers over the years during motorcycle week. Smoke from the campers' fires often filled the sky over Mount Belknap. Many locals left their homes and camped out at the area during motorcycle week so as not to miss out on any fun. (Courtesy of Butch Baer.)

Pictured here are members of the Springfield Motorcycle Club. They are camping at the Belknap Recreation Area during motorcycle week. From left to right are Edmond Picard, Harry Gagner, Priscilla Gagner, Ron Mainville, and Charlie Coles. Their AMA banner hangs in the trees behind them. (Courtesy of Butch Baer.)

Riding contests were a big part of the AMA's gypsy tours. Laconia was no exception. This game of skill, riding the plank, was set up in the rear parking lot at Belknap Recreation Area. The judge pays very close attention to the contestants in this Eric Sanford photograph. These contests were very trying in the rain. (Courtesy of Butch Baer.)

Shown here in this Sanford photograph, another riding contest, held at the main parking lot at Belknap Recreation Area, is throwing a ring onto a pole while in motion. The wet ground made it even more of a challenge. The crowd cheered with every successful throw. (Courtesy of Butch Baer.)

34

Other popular contests during motorcycle week were the look-alike contest and the best-dressed contest for motorcycle clubs. In the 1940s and most of the 1950s, most of the contests were held at the Belknap Recreation Area. In the late 1950s, the contests were moved to Weirs Beach. Pictured here in this 1955 Bob St. Louis photograph is the Blais family at the look-alike contest. Judging from the crowds watching, the winners of the contests were widely admired. (Courtesy of Butch Baer.)

The members of a motorcycle club were at attention while being judged for their uniforms at the lodge at Belknap Recreation Area. The clubs took these contests very seriously. The winners often brought their trophy to all motorcycle events they attended. (Courtesy of Butch Baer.)

Fred Marsh presents a trophy to a winning motorcycle club in the lodge at Belknap Recreation Area. Fritzie Baer can be seen announcing the winners in the rear of the photograph wearing his famous red hat. The members all wore riding boots that were meticulously shined. There were no cash prizes although the trophies were coveted. (Courtesy of Butch Baer.)

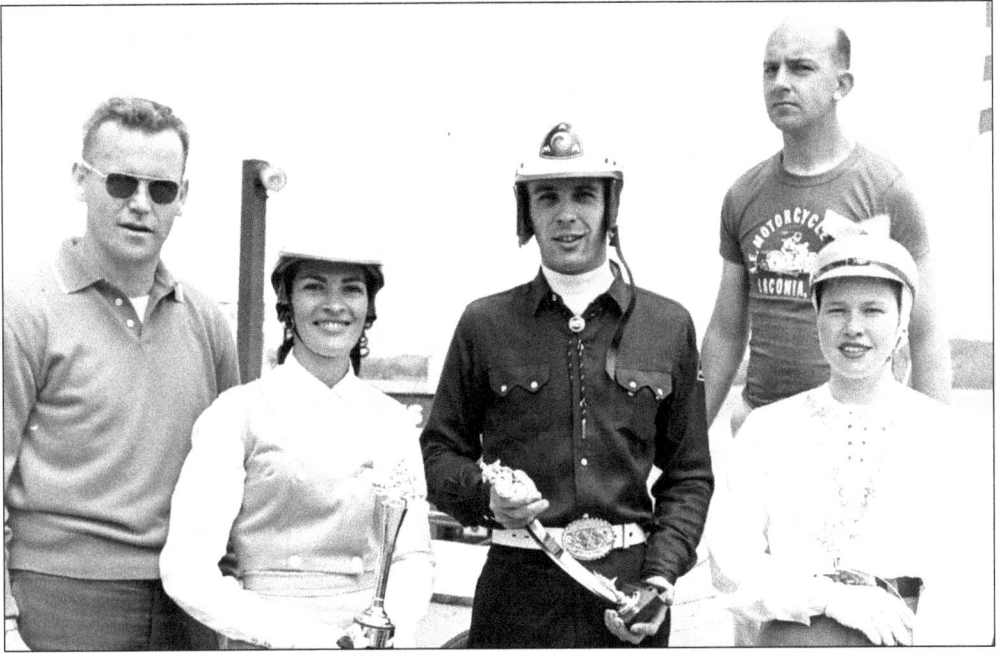

This group of winners pose with their trophies at Weirs Beach at the completion of a gypsy tour contest. The rider with the AMA logo on his helmet also has the AMA patch on his left sleeve. Being a member of the AMA was a source of pride for many riders in the 1940s and the 1950s. (Courtesy of Butch Baer.)

By the mid-1950s, most of the uniform contests had been moved from Belknap Recreation Area to Lakeside Avenue or onto the boardwalk in Weirs Beach. These contests were often held on Friday or Saturday mornings. The motorcycle clubs involved took these contests very seriously. The group at the far end of Lakeside Avenue is posing in front of their motorcycles. (Courtesy of Butch Baer.)

For many not-for-profit organizations, motorcycle week was and is a great chance to raise money. In the lodge at the Belknap Recreation Area, Fritzie Baer announces to the crowd to pitch in for the March of Dimes in 1955. Also seen in this Bob St. Louis photograph is New Hampshire governor Lane Dwinell, second from right. (Courtesy of Butch Baer.)

A Columbia bicycle provides a ride for this young girl on the track at Belknap Recreation Area to help raise funds for the March of Dimes in 1957. The crowd is paying close attention to the youngster. This was done before the start of the last big race. Note the AMA patch on the official on the right. (Courtesy of Laconia Historical Society.)

Bill Schietinger (left) from the New England Motorcycle Dealers Association presents a check to B. Parker of the Laconia Hospital in this Earl H. Wells photograph. Fritzie Baer is looking on. The money was raised during motorcycle week. Each year, money that was raised was given to such programs like the Laconia Hospital Fund, the Laconia Nursing School, and other Laconia charities. (Courtesy of Butch Baer.)

In 1946, radio was the predominant way to reach the public with live, on the spot news. Here Baer, on the far right, waits for the show discussing the up and coming gypsy tour and races. Some of the others in the group are Dot Robinson (standing, middle), members of the Motor Maids, Lt. John Lockwood of the New Hampshire State Police (second from right) and Ted Edwards (third from left). (Courtesy of Butch Baer.)

This photograph is of the gypsy tour in 1957 at Belknap Recreation Area on a sunny day. From left to right are Jules Horry from the American Motorcycle Association; Earl Robinson; Dot Robinson, president of the Motor Maids; and Fritzie Baer. Dot rode her motorcycle to Laconia from her home in Michigan every year. Note that running lights are no longer on top of the fender of this newer Harley-Davidson. (Courtesy of Butch Baer.)

Photographer Norman R. Brady was in the right spot at the right time to catch this group of BMW riders in the parking area just north of the main lodge at Belknap Recreation Area. The BMW Riders of America held rallies during motorcycle week in Laconia for years. The main camping area for Belknap Recreation Area is straight ahead to the right. (Courtesy of Wayne L. Caveney.)

Fritzie Baer (standing, left), manager of the Belknap Recreation Area, is joined by attorney Paul Normandin (standing, right) and three members of the Belknap County Commissioners in this photograph taken by Loran Percy on a winter day. Planning for the gypsy tour and 100-Mile National Championship Road Races went on year-round. Now that Baer was the manager of the Belknap Recreation Area, there were people in the motorcycle week loop like never before. (Courtesy of Butch Baer.)

In 1957, the catch phrase for the "World Greatest Gypsy Tour" was "7 in '57." Another planning session is being held, and this time it is at the Greater Laconia Weirs Beach Chamber of Commerce office in the Laconia Tavern. Standing from left to right are Fritzie Baer, Paul McKinney, Roy Van Etten, and Robert Funesti. Peter Karagianis, who continues to be active today in his support for Laconia Motorcycle Week, is seated. (Courtesy of Butch Baer.)

By 1959, many businesses in the center of New Hampshire looked forward to the increase of business brought by motorcycle week. Here Fritzie Baer, second from the left, is presented a silver bowl by Ed Hoagland on behalf of the Weirs Beach Publicity Bureau. This was in recognition for all the work Baer did for the area. Standing between Baer and Hoagland is Baer's wife, Louise. To the right of Hoagland are Laconia mayor Ollie Huot and Jim Irwin. (Courtesy of Butch Baer.)

This photograph shows a group discussing final plans for the 1958 road races and gypsy tour. From left to right are (first row) Bill Schietinger, Peter Karagianis, and Archie Brown of the New Hampshire State Police; (second row) Charlie Burdill, Laconia police chief Mickey Dunleavy, Fritzie Baer, and George Kerguey of the New Hampshire State Police. Note the motorcycle week logo in the poster. This logo was changed in 1993 to add a female rider. (Courtesy of Butch Baer.)

Here is Dick Muzzy standing in front of his beloved lavender Harley-Davidson Panhead during motorcycle week in 1959. Note the chrome stallion on the front fender. It is thought that Muzzy had the only lavender motorcycle in the area. As is common today, most riders like to make their motorcycles a little unique. The gypsy tours were a great chance to show off to your peers. (Courtesy of Pat Muzzy.)

40th ANNUAL NEW ENGLAND GYPSY TOUR
JUNE 13, 14, 15, 16, 17, 18, 19, 1960
BELKNAP MOUNTAIN RECREATION AREA, LACONIA, N. H.

100-MILE NATIONAL CHAMPIONSHIP MOTORCYCLE ROAD RACE SUNDAY, JUNE 19 $6350 Cash Prize Money	Sponsored by Greater Laconia and Weirs Beach Chamber of Commerce and New England Motorcycle Dealers' Association, Inc.	50-MILE CHAMPIONSHIP MOTORCYCLE ROAD RACE SUNDAY, JUNE 19 CHAMPIONSHIP NOVICE ROAD RACE — SATURDAY, JUNE 18

The year 1960 saw the 40th gypsy tour coming to Laconia and the 18th year of the 100-Mile National Championship Road Races. As their advertising shows, Laconia was the biggest rally in the country in 1960, with all the motorcycle companies being here and all of the big name racers of the time making the ride to Laconia. (Courtesy of Butch Baer.)

The closing day parade travels to Belknap Recreation Area down Laconia's Main Street on the last day of motorcycle week. The parade stretches all the way north toward Opechee Park where it begins. The parade route is about 12 miles long with large crowds watching on all the downtown streets. (Courtesy of Raymond Reed.)

Many riders made their way to the downtown area to be in town for the early Sunday morning parade to Belknap Recreation Area. Many without rooms ended up sleeping on the Laconia Library lawn or the lawn of private homes near Opechee Park. Some residents were not pleased by this but others brought out coffee to their surprised outdoor home guests. (Courtesy of Raymond Reed.)

From here, the south entrance to Belknap Recreation Area, the participants of the gypsy tour parade of motorcycle week entered the area. Here they all parked in neat lines for Sunday's big 100-mile National Championship Road Race. There were always several hundred motorcycles in the final gypsy tour parade. (Courtesy of Butch Baer.)

42nd ANNUAL NEW ENGLAND

GYPSY TOUR

A.M.A. SANCTIONED NATIONAL CHAMPIONSHIP

MOTORCYCLE ROAD RACES

LACONIA, NEW HAMPSHIRE

1962 Red Hat Brigade of the Greater Laconia - Weirs Beach Chamber of Commerce

These are the men and women who sacrificed time and energy from their own businesses to raise the money needed to sponsor this year's Motorcycle Week. These men will be wearing their famous Red Hats while you are in the Laconia Area. Seated left to right; Ron Rhinehart, Carroll Stafford, Jr., Bol Holbrook, Bill Lyman, Harold Richardson, Ben Zulofsky and Norvin Laubenstein. Standing left to right; Louise Morse, Chamber of Commerce Secretary, Parker C. Lindberg, Chamber of Commerce Manager, Phil Droste, Fritzie Baer, Peter Makris, Hal Gunn and Jim Dodge.

OFFICIAL PROGRAM

Auspices of New England Motorcycle Dealers' Assn.

JUNE 12 thru 17, 1962

PRICE 50c

This cover of the official program of the 1962 gypsy tour and 100-Mile National Championship Road Race shows the who's who of the Red Hat Brigade. The funds raised by the Red Hat Brigade were used to help fund motorcycle week. Today the fund-raising to support the Laconia Motorcycle Week Association is done through corporate sponsorship, the state of New Hampshire's Joint Promotional Program grant, and today's version of the Red Hat Brigade—the Rally Patrons. This money allows the association to promote the rally and the state of New Hampshire year-round at other rallies and at trade shows throughout the country. (Courtesy of Laconia Motorcycle Week Association.)

46

Two

Road Races at Belknap Recreation Area

Motorcycle racing, hill climbs, and drag racing were happening at Laconia right from the first year of the gypsy tour. With no courses for these events to take place, they were often held wherever they could be safely done.

Tower Hill at Weirs Beach was famous for riders racing their motorcycles up the hill. Motorcycle races were held between riders anywhere the road was good. That all changed in 1938 when a man named Fritzie Baer and the New England Motorcycle Dealers Association worked together to bring the AMA-sanctioned 200-Mile National Championship Races to Belknap Recreation Area located in Gilford, near Laconia. The next year in 1939, the National Championship Road Race was changed from a 200 mile to a 100 mile race because of the length and time the 200 mile race took.

Belknap Recreation Area held the hill climbs, drag races, scrambles, and many other motorcycle-related contests. During the war years of 1942 through 1945, the gypsy tour and road races were cancelled. However, by 1946, there was a jump in enthusiasts and attendance for the races. Laconia Motorcycle Week continued to prosper through the 1950s, but the 1960s brought changes in the way some elected officials viewed motorcycle week.

The last hill climbs at Belknap Recreation Area were in 1962 and would not come back until 1993. The last road races at Belknap were held until 1963 and were then moved to Bryar Motor Sports Park.

This is the view from the top of the 70-meter ski jump hill, which was used for the hill climbs at Belknap Recreation Area. This shows a nice view of the rider just reaching the top. In 1962, the county commissioners were in the process of scaling back activities at Belknap Recreation Area for various reasons. Some felt that the crowds now being attracted to the area were getting a little rowdy, especially in the evening hours. Others felt that the hill climb was not pulling its weight with regards to income. Because of these various reasons, 1962 was the last year for sanctioned hill climbs. After a lot of hard work, various staff members of Gunstock Mountain Resort (formerly Belknap) led by Sylvia Legget were able to bring the hill climbs back to Gunstock in 1993. After a 30-year absence, a sunny day can bring over 10,000 fans to watch the hill climbs. (Courtesy of Raymond Reed.)

This photograph shows the view from the base of the 70-meter ski jump used for the hill climbs at Belknap Recreation Area. The dust trail shows the location of the hill climber. The hill climb was not always held at the ski jump. It was also held on the Phelps Trail, which is located by the main lodge. For most viewers and participants, the ski jump is the favorite location for the hill climb. The steepness of the hill adds to the excitement. (Courtesy of Raymond Reed.)

Hill climbs have remained the mainstay of rallies and motorcycle events all over the world. The look of determination on this rider's face says it all. For most, the adrenaline rush of making it to the top made all of the work well worth it. This rider's motorcycle, No. 234, looks like a stock Triumph unlike many of the modified motorcycles hill climbers would use. (Courtesy of Raymond Reed.)

In the 1950s and early 1960s, the hill climbs were done on a year-long accumulated point system to determine the winners. Now the climbers are either categorized as amateur or professional, and they have a great time in their class trying to win a trophy. Many of the riders belonged to the New England Hill Climbers. There is a class for young riders under the age of 18 and there is also a class for all-terrain vehicles (ATVs). This climber has made it to the top of the hill. He may be the winner in his class if no one else beats his time going to the top. (Courtesy of Raymond Reed.)

To win the hill climb, it is not just getting to the top; a rider must also be the fastest. This rider in the 1940s is well on his way to making good time without much gear. Riders today have all kinds of safety gear, including helmets, chest protectors, padded gloves, and reinforced boots. All of this gear adds to the difficulty of making good time up the hill. (Courtesy of Raymond Reed.)

This rider in the early 1950s may not have made it to the top. Not making it to the top means the rider has to ride or walk their motorcycle back down the hill, which is no small feat because of the sharp incline of the hill. Note the chains on the rear tire. Not all hill climbers use this practice. Some rear tires had a form of paddles to help gain traction up the hill. (Courtesy of Raymond Reed.)

Another rider breaks the crest of the hill. In the 1940s and the 1950s, hill climbers came from all around the United States to compete at Laconia. When the hill climbs were cancelled after 1962, it certainly was not because of a lack of support but more from a changing regime and attitude of the Belknap County Commissioners that were in charge of Belknap Recreation Area. (Courtesy of Raymond Reed.)

The national championship motorcycle road races in New England were first held in Keene and then at Old Orchard Beach in Maine. Fritzie Baer, along with the New England Motorcycle Dealers Association, made all the right moves to get the races moved to Belknap Recreation Area for the 1938 gypsy tour. The 1938 gypsy tour and races were held from September 8 through the 11. In 1939, they were held from June 22 through the 25. (Courtesy of Butch Baer.)

Fritzie Baer is standing third from the left with many of the staff and supporters of the New England Motorcycle Dealers Association before the start of the first 200-Mile National Championship Road Race at Belknap Recreation Area on September 11, 1938. The start of the race was the result of almost two years of collaboration to move the race from Old Orchard Beach, Maine, to Belknap Recreation Area. (Courtesy of Butch Baer.)

Edward Lydiard, on the right, is seen here in 1938 presenting the winning trophy in the best-dressed club contest to a member of the Rhode Island Ramblers Motorcycle Club. Lydiard worked with John Zimmerman from Keene to help Baer bring the national championship road races to Belknap Recreation Area in 1938. (Courtesy of Butch Baer.)

A group of motorcyclists line up in front of Cantin's Chevrolet garage on Union Avenue in Laconia in the early 1950s. During the gypsy tour, many of the service stations and car dealers on Union Avenue were very busy with oil changes, tire sales, and lots of gasoline being sold. Others held bike washes for the visitors. Many stayed open extra hours to handle the increase in business. (Courtesy of Raymond Reed.)

Lined up for a photograph before the start of the 100-Mile National Championship Road Races in 1941 are four of the racers from that year. From left to right are Alli Quatrocci, James Lewter, June McCall, and Doug Creech. No one knew it but this would be the last race at Belknap Recreation Area until 1946 because of the attack on Pearl Harbor and the United States entering World War II. (Courtesy of Butch Baer.)

Two racers are neck and neck as they ride by one of the few buildings on the race course at Belknap Recreation Area. The building was reserved for members of the AMA, judges, members of the New England Motorcycle Dealers Association, or staff members of the Belknap Recreation Area. Note the few bales of hay in front of the building. (Courtesy of Butch Baer.)

With the end of World War II, everyone was just happy to be alive and back to the things they enjoyed the most. The faces of these riders and their crew say it all. Two of the racers identified here in 1946 before the start of the 100-Mile National Championship Road Race at Belknap Recreation Area are George Sabine on the No. 20 bike and Terry Edwards on the No. 13 bike. (Courtesy of Butch Baer.)

There was much happiness in 1946 with the resumption of the New England gypsy tour and the 100-Mile National Championship Road Races at Laconia and at Belknap Recreation Area. World War II had been over for almost a year and many events were back on schedule. Many of those who were part of the racing circuit served in the armed forces during the war. The popularity of motorcycles took off after the war as hundreds of thousands were released from the service. Many new motorcycle clubs were formed around the nation. Membership in the AMA began to grow and businesses around Laconia and the Lakes Region were happy to see the return of the motorcyclists and the business they brought. Pictured here from left to right are Anne and Ted Edwards on No. 13, Bill Anderson on No. 8, two unidentified, Alli Qualtrocki on No. 29, Fritzie Baer, C. Smith, Ed Kretz on No. 1, and unidentified. (Courtesy of Butch Baer.)

Here in 1940, Baer and his brother Carl pose for a publicity shot with the AMA trophies, which are for the winning placers at the 100-Mile National Championship Road Races at Laconia. All of the racers were sanctioned by the AMA. Carl did not work on the motorcycle races but took part in the fun at Laconia. (Courtesy of Butch Baer.)

This postcard photograph shows the start of the 100-Mile National Championship Road Race in 1946. Some of those pictured here are Ben Campanale on No. 2, Bill Anderson on No. 8, Ted Edwards on No. 13, Ed Kretz on No. 1, Jim Chann on No. 16, Bill Miller on No. 14, and Albert Wolfe on No. 12. Note the crowd of spectators along the course in the top right of the photograph. (Courtesy of Butch Baer.)

This photograph was used by the advertising department of the Indian Motorcycle Company of Springfield, Massachusetts. It was taken in 1946 and is of the 100-Mile National Championship Road Race in Laconia. Of interest to the Indian Motorcycle Company was Alli Qualtrocki on No. 34, who was riding his Indian motorcycle. Also pictured is Leon Newhall on No. 48, John Butterfield on No. 77, and Babe Tancrede on No. 21. All of the racers had steel plates fitted to their boots for use on the dirt track. (Courtesy of Butch Baer.)

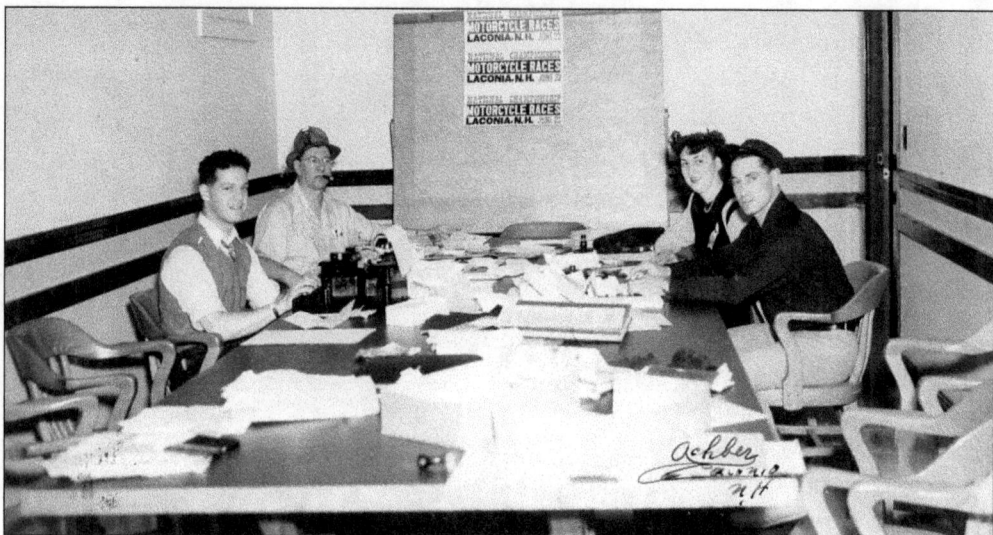

The year 1946 also saw an increase in the amount of publicity and advertising that was done to increase awareness in the general public that the New England gypsy tour and 100-Mile National Championship Road Races were back on in Laconia and at Belknap Recreation Area. A big supporter of the motorcycle events during the gypsy tour was Edward S. Gallagher, who was with the local newspaper, the *Laconia Evening Citizen*. Seen here from left to right are Sam Clevenson, who was the sports writer for the *Laconia Evening Citizen*; Fritzie Baer; Barbara Lyman; and Bud Acker. They are going over the plans for 1946 gypsy tour. (Courtesy of Butch Baer.)

Tickets for the 100-Mile National Championship Road Races were sold at different locations around Laconia just before and during the New England gypsy tour. In this photograph by Loran Percy, the ticket booth was just next to the main lodge at the Belknap Recreation Area. Seen in the booth from left to right are Gert Schietinger, Mr. and Mrs. Bill Schietinger, and Mrs. Schietinger's sisters. (Courtesy of Butch Baer.)

Prior to the start of the 100-Mile National Championship Races at Belknap Recreation Area, the Motor Maids of America lead a parade around the course of the race. The Motor Maids were a big part of the races and the gypsy tour. The idea for the Motor Maids began with discussions at Laconia in 1939. (Courtesy of Butch Baer.)

As No. 58 gets the checkered flag at the end of the Laconia 100-Mile National Championship Road Race at Belknap Recreation Area, Baer, on the right with his clipboard in hand and his red hat on tight, can barely contain his excitement on the side of the course in this Loran Percy photograph. The end of the race and another successful Laconia Motorcycle Week meant the world to Baer and his staff. (Courtesy of Butch Baer.)

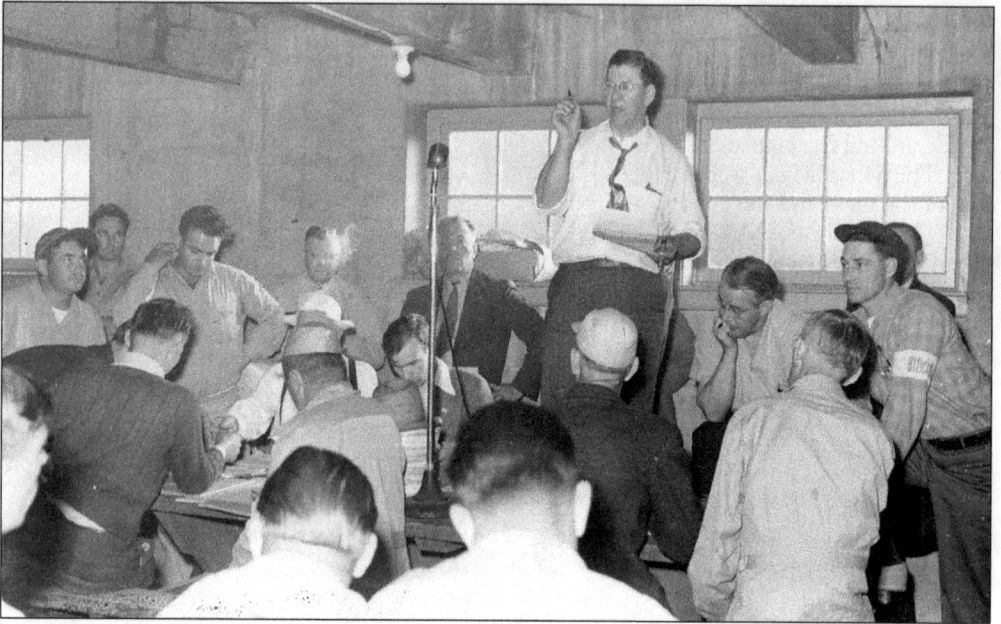

In 1946, Fritzie Baer gave a speech during a rider's meeting at Belknap Recreation Area just before the last day of races. Also included in the meeting are the judges and officials of the race. This is a rare photograph of Baer without his red hat on. All of the rules set by the AMA had to be followed to the letter. Any infraction could cause a rider to be disqualified. (Courtesy of Butch Baer.)

This is a very small section of the crowd watching the 100-Mile National Championship Road Races at Belknap Recreation Area. The crowd here is 20 to 30 people deep in spots. Everyone loved to be at the hairpin turns or on the straightaways. When the race was first held at Belknap Recreation Area in 1938, it was a 200-mile race, which took up to five hours to complete. The next year it was changed to a 100-mile race because of the length of time. (Courtesy of Butch Baer.)

Here is the starting line for the races at Belknap Recreation Area. The area behind the building is restricted to officials only. To the left of the photograph is the location for the hill climbs on the 70-meter ski jump. To the right in the photograph is the famous hairpin turn. To the rear of the photograph is where the motorcycles that rode from Laconia to Belknap in the gypsy tour parade are parked. (Courtesy of Butch Baer.)

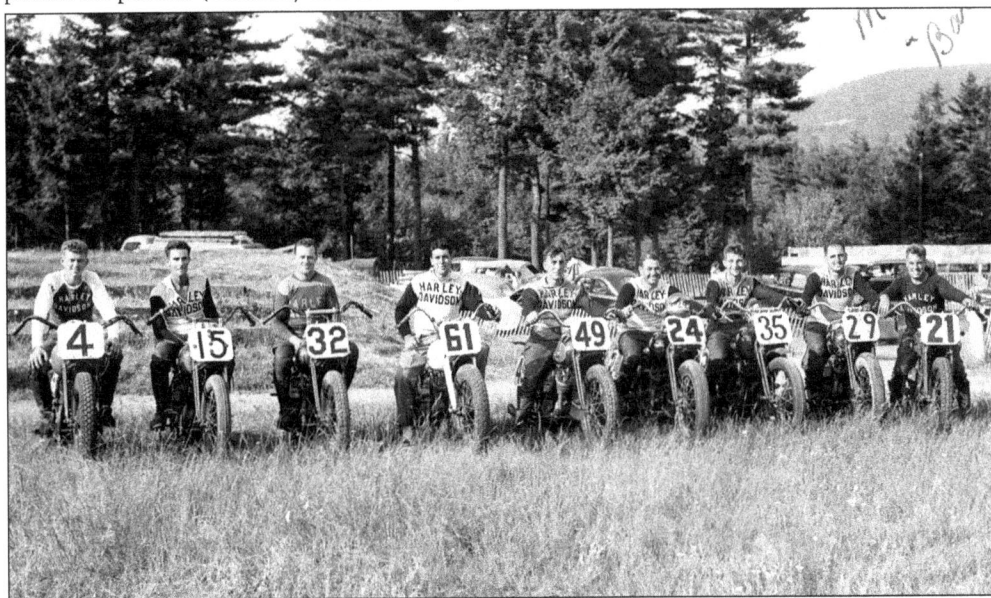

This Norman P. Speirs photograph shows part of the line up for the Laconia 100-Mile National Championship Road Races in 1949. Since all of the riders are on Harley-Davidsons, the shot was probably for the public relations department of the Harley-Davidson Motor Company. From left to right are "Little" Joe Weatherly on No. 4, Win Young on No. 15, Miller McDonner on No. 32, "Sal" Scirpo on No. 61, Ray Angstadt on No. 49, "Buck" Brigance on No. 24, Bill Miller on No. 35, Stan Myers on No. 29, and Arthur "Babe" Tancrede on No. 21. (Courtesy of Butch Baer.)

By 1950, Fritzie Baer, seen here standing on the right, had been hired as the manager of Belknap Recreation Area. To accept this job, Baer had to leave the Indian Motorcycle Company where he had worked for 30 years and move his family to Laconia from Massachusetts. One of his first accomplishments was to improve the course over which the 100-Mile National Championship Road Races were held. (Courtesy of Butch Baer.)

Since much of the course used in the 100-Mile National Championship Road Races at Belknap Recreation Area was dirt, paving only made sense. It was a great course, but paving improved both safety and speed during the races. Seen here with Baer (far left) are members of the Belknap County Commissioners, who had to approve major decisions regarding Belknap Recreation Area. (Courtesy of Butch Baer.)

This is the junction of Gilford Avenue and Union Avenue in Laconia. This is also the route that the big gypsy tour parade took to get to Belknap Recreation Area on the last day of the gypsy tour after riding through downtown Laconia. This Peter Besh photograph is from 1951. Today the elm trees that lined Gilford Avenue are gone as is the large sign on the left listing what was happening at the Belknap Recreation Area. (Courtesy of the Laconia Motorcycle Week Association.)

Weddings such as the one held here at the Belknap Recreation Area during motorcycle week in 1956 were big attractions for the motorcyclists attending the rally. The groom and the bride (behind him) are getting ready to do a lap around the race course. Some years right after World War II ended, as many as 50 weddings took place during motorcycle week. (Courtesy of Butch Baer.)

In this 1950 photograph taken by W. E. Huntington, Fritzie Baer sits on his motorcycle at Belknap Recreation Area. With him, from left to right, are Violet Thayer, E. C. Smith, and Ed Fuller. It was not often that Baer was seen in a suit. Missing is his cigar, but he does have his red hat on and a pencil behind his right ear. (Courtesy of Butch Baer.)

Photographer Bob St. Louis has caught the front of the pack during the 100-Mile National Championship Road Race at Belknap Recreation Area. The chain link fence is all that stands between the spectators and the racers. Accidents involving spectators and racers were very rare but did happen. (Courtesy of Butch Baer.)

Over the years, many members of the federal government and Hollywood's famous were seen at Laconia enjoying the AMA gypsy tour and the 100-Mile National Championship Road Race at Belknap Recreation Area. The man at the far right is Eddie "Rochester" Anderson, who was a star on the Jack Benny Show. Sitting on his motorcycle is Bobby Hill, the 25-mile national championship race winner in 1951. He also won in 1952. Baer stands between the two. At the far left is Sherwood Dixon, lieutenant governor of Illinois. (Courtesy of Butch Baer.)

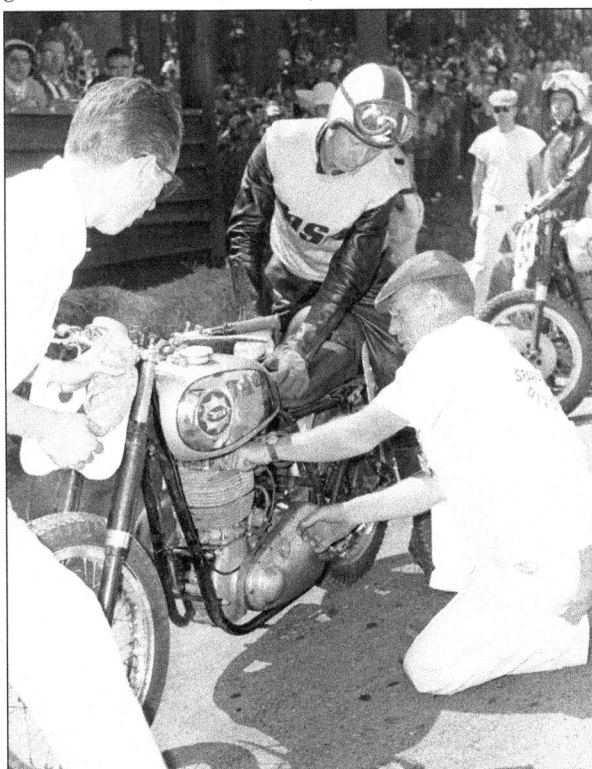

This photograph, taken by Bob St. Louis, shows racer Dick Klamfoth sitting on his BSA motorcycle. The motorcycle is being fine-tuned before the start of the national race at Belknap Recreation Area in 1954. In the back of this photograph is Sammy Tanner, racer No. 59, standing next to his motorcycle. Klamfoth won the championship races at Laconia several times and also won races at the championship races in Daytona Beach, Florida. Klamfoth says his best races were on BSA or Norton motorcycles. He still races on occasion today. (Courtesy of Butch Baer.)

The importance of motorcycle week in Laconia was not lost on many elected officials around the state of New Hampshire. In this photograph, New Hampshire governor Hugh Gregg is seen sitting on a Norton motorcycle with Fritzie Baer standing next to him at the Norton display in the lodge at the Belknap Recreation Area in 1953 during motorcycle week. Gregg spent as much time as he could both at Weirs Beach and at Belknap Recreation Area during motorcycle week. (Courtesy of Butch Baer.)

In this photograph by Peter Besh, Gregg appears with Baer in the lodge during motorcycle week in 1954. The official pin, which Baer has on his red hat, was worn by all who worked the races and contest held at the "area," which is what many people called the Belknap Recreation Area. It is unknown who the bottle of Ruppert Knickerbocker beer seen at the lower left belongs to. (Courtesy of Butch Baer.)

While the prize money was important to the winners of the races, the trophies were just as important. Some of the large trophies had the names of the winners engraved on the trophy year after year. This was called a revolving trophy. Seen here on the right in this photograph by Bob St. Louis is Brad Andres, the winner in 1955 at the Laconia nationals held at Belknap Recreation Area. Andres is holding the Laconia Wynn Oil trophy. On his left is his father, Leonard, holding the 100-Mile National Championship trophy. (Courtesy of Butch Baer.)

The time keepers had a tough job at races such as Laconia. Here the time keepers on the right are timing the races during the 25- and 50-mile amateur races at Belknap Recreation Area. This photograph by Eric Sanford also catches the race officials dressed in white gathered by the finish line. Bob Finn is in the striped shirt. (Courtesy of Butch Baer.)

Photographer Bob St. Louis shows manager Fritzie Baer congratulating Brad Andres after the race that he won in 1955. Behind them, the fans are jammed tight to be in on the excitement of the winner. Baer has the "I like motorcycles" button on his red hat, his stop watch around his neck, and the ever-present cigar in his right hand. (Courtesy of Butch Baer.)

The lodge at Belknap Recreation Area was the center of activities during motorcycle week. This photograph by Eric Sanford shows some of the action outside the lodge. With factory displays in the lodge and ticket sales just outside it, lines can be seen forming outside the entrance of the lodge. (Courtesy of Butch Baer.)

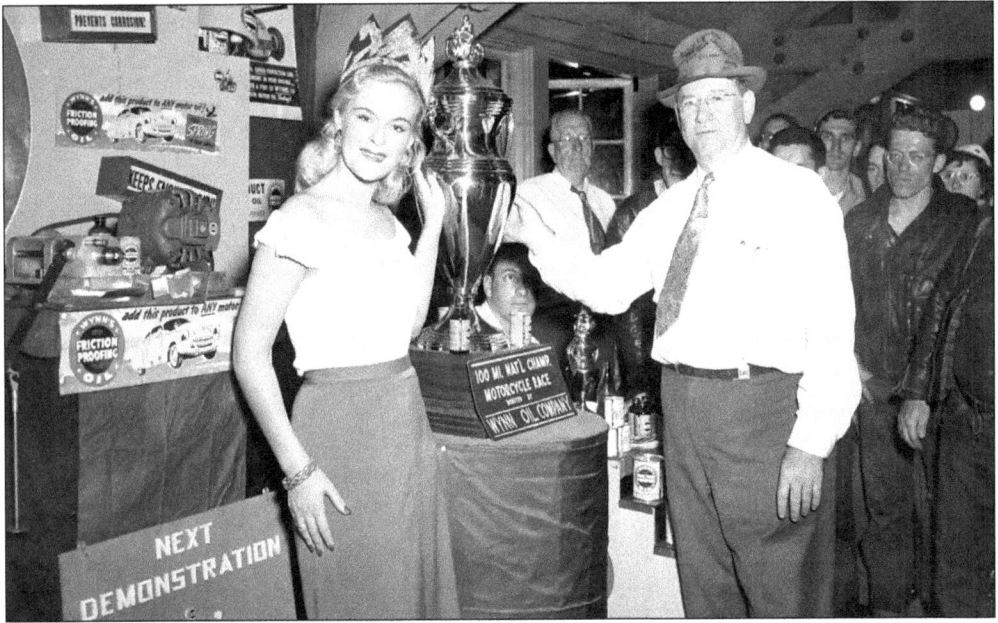

Fitzie Baer poses with Miss Wynn Oil and the Wynn Oil trophy, which was given to the winner of the 100-Mile National Championship Road Race at Laconia. Wynn Oil was a major sponsor of the races at Belknap Recreation Area for a number of years in the 1950s and 1960s. The ever-present crowd stands off to the rear of Baer to watch the pictures being taken. (Courtesy of Butch Baer.)

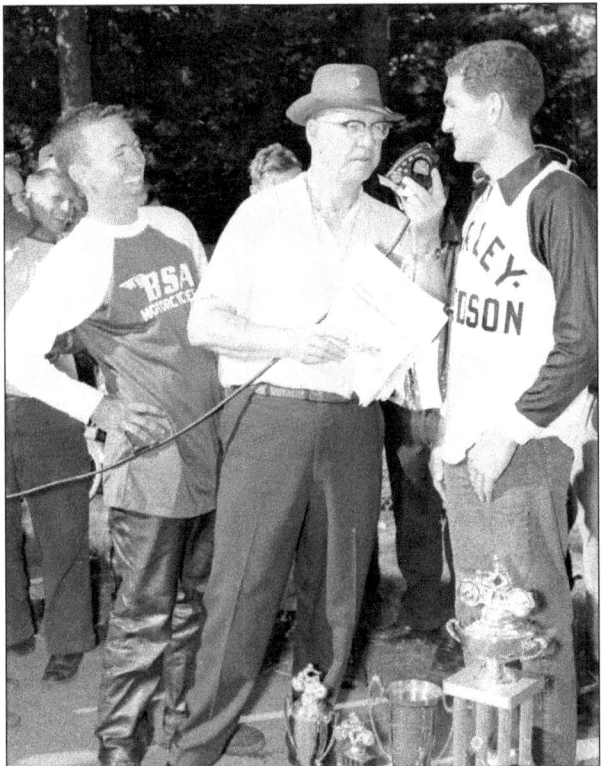

This photograph, taken by St. Louis, shows Baer holding the radio microphone for a live radio broadcast after the last race in 1956. The local AM station, WLNH, carried a lot of the action live from Belknap Recreation Area. Many businesses in Laconia had their radio dials turned up so everyone could hear the action taking place at the area. (Courtesy of Butch Baer.)

Bobby Labrie was a well-known fixture at Laconia during the gypsy tour and 100-Mile National Championship Road Races at Belknap Recreation Area. Labrie's father ran the Harley-Davidson dealership in Concord for years, giving him the chance to spend his youth around motorcycles. Labrie soon became an ace mechanic with racers and racing teams stopping by his own motorcycle shop to work on their bikes with him. Labrie participated in the drag races that were held at Belknap Recreation Area during motorcycle week. The races were normally held on Thursday during the rally. He broke and still holds one of the records for the drag race today. In this photograph, he can be seen on the right, leaning on the trailer that his dragster is loaded onto and is getting ready to head up to Belknap. Labrie passed away in 1997. (Courtesy of Bev Labrie.)

Seen in this 1958 Bob St. Louis photograph, from left to right, are Bill Schietinger; Fritzie Baer; 100-Mile National Championship Road Race winner Roger Reiman; Baer's son Bobby, who was an assistant manager at Belknap Recreation Area; and Reiman's father, Hank. Bobby was on the racing circuit before World War II. He served on an aircraft carrier flight crew during the war. After the war, he continued to race Indian motorcycles. (Courtesy of Butch Baer.)

This photograph by Loran Percy catches the action after the hairpin turn on the course during one of the AMA-sanctioned races at Belknap Recreation Area during motorcycle week. At the right is the officials' building. Also to the right is the 70-meter ski jump, the site for the AMA-sanctioned hill climbs. The crowd is packed tight against the chain-link fence, which separates the crowd from the course. (Courtesy of Butch Baer.)

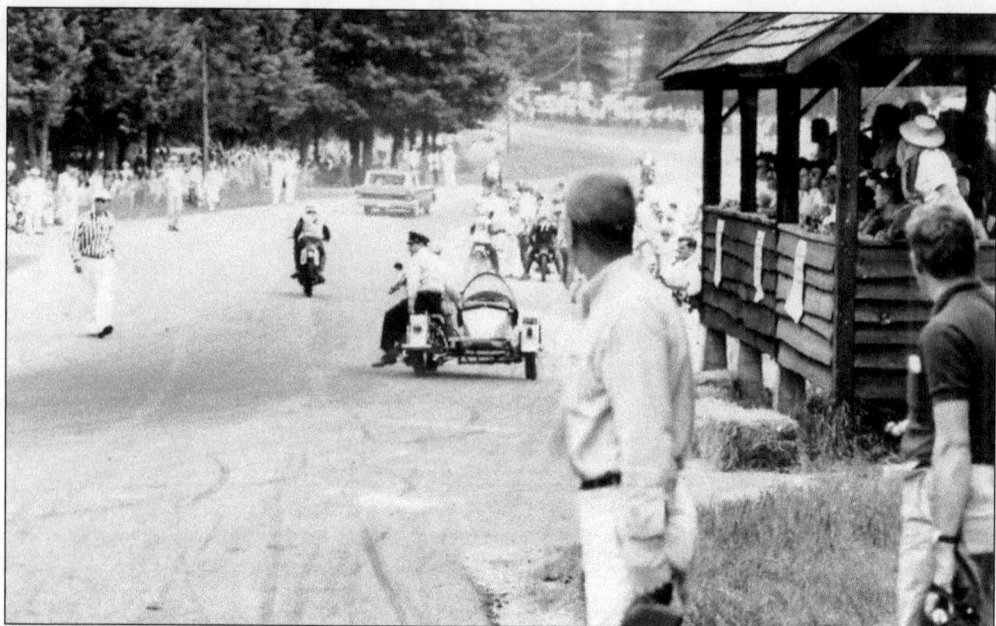

Racer Dick Klamfoth, on No. 2, follows an ambulance on the track as it races towards the scene of an accident. There were accidents every year during the races. Most accidents resulted in broken bones at worst. In 1962, a motorcycle somehow jumped the fence and landed on a young boy who retained serious injuries. After a long delay, the races were resumed. (Courtesy of Butch Baer.)

Fritzie Baer is standing on the right next to Roger Reiman in this 1958 photograph. On the other side of Reiman is his father, Hank. Quite often, parents and siblings of racers attended the races at the Belknap Recreation Area. It was not unusual for one or both of the parents to stand with the racer during a photo opportunity. (Courtesy of Butch Baer.)

This photograph by Eric Sanford shows the gypsy tour parade riding through downtown Laconia on Main Street on its way to Belknap Recreation Area in 1955. The gentleman on top of the step ladder has positioned himself in a great spot to take pictures. On Sunday morning, the participants in the last parade of the rally gathered at Opechee Park on North Main Street. Spectators lined the route from Opechee Park down North Main Street to Main Street, up Union Avenue, and then onto Gilford Avenue to the Belknap Recreation Area. (Courtesy of Butch Baer.)

In the late 1950s, sisters Donna Lawton (left) and Sandra Lawton pose with the 100-Mile National Championship Road Race Wynn Oil winner's trophy. The Lawton family owned and operated Funspot at Weirs Beach and were a big part of motorcycle week in the late 1950s through 1965. The Lawtons were also instrumental in helping to bring back motorcycle week from a weekend in 1991. (Courtesy of the Weirs Times.)

In this 1958 photograph, the trophies are all ready to be handed out. This many trophies today would cost several thousand dollars. A motorcyclist still has a chance to win trophies today at the various bike shows, flat-track races, hill climbs, vintage races, and at the Loudon Classic. This photograph is at the lodge at Belknap Recreation Area. There is a poster on the back wall which says it is the 20th anniversary, which is for the actual road races, not the AMA gypsy tour. (Courtesy of Butch Baer.)

Bill Schietinger is seen here holding a trophy on the side of the race course at Belknap Recreation Area. He was a very familiar face at Laconia during motorcycle week. He was the owner of two Harley-Davidson dealerships in Connecticut. He was also very active in the New England Motorcycle Dealers Association, which helped sponsor the New England AMA gypsy tour and the 100-Mile National Championship Road Races. For all of his work with motorcycle week, Schietinger was made, at one point, honorary mayor for the city of Laconia. (Courtesy of Butch Baer.)

Manager Fritzie Baer is taking a much-needed break during a race at Belknap Recreation Area. The picture shows a cloud of cigar smoke hovering in front of him and also on the ground in front of his clipboard. Baer used his clipboard to help keep track of the racers. Baer's term as manager at Belknap Recreation Area ended in 1960. But that did not end his work with motorcycle week at Laconia. (Courtesy of Butch Baer.)

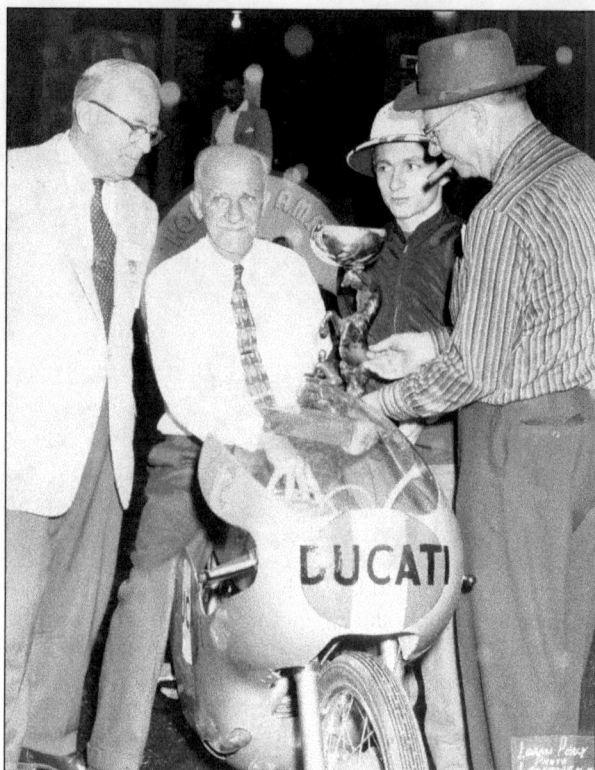

By 1960, there were many foreign motorcycle brands in the races at Belknap Recreation Area during motorcycle week. Here Fritzie Baer, on the right, presents the Fritzie Baer Sportsman Trophy to Italian rider Franco Farne, who made the trip to Laconia to take part in the 100-Mile National Championship Road Race. On the far left are Bill Schietinger and Oril Steele, both of the New England Harley-Davidson Dealers Association. The Ducati motorcycle company from Italy has since become a force in motorcycle racing. (Courtesy of Butch Baer.)

This postcard photograph shows a perfect shot of the starting flag for the race at Belknap Recreation Area during motorcycle week. Other activities that took place at the area during motorcycle week were motorcycle scrambles held on Tuesday, the international motorcycle shows that ran all week, the hill climb on Wednesday, drag races on Thursday, movies in the lodge, lightweight motorcycle races, contests and other added events on Friday, and then novice races on Saturday. The whole week was certainly action packed. (Courtesy of Wayne Caveney.)

This photograph by Bob St. Louis shows the racing action at a halt. This motorcycle is totally engulfed in flames caused by a punctured gas tank. Fires of this magnitude were not usual. The fuel used for the races, the drags, and the hill climbs was of the highest octane that could be found. (Courtesy of Laconia Historical Society.)

The official with the flag continues to hold the race while the fire is put out with the help of two fire extinguishers. At today's races, most tracks have their own fire trucks and crews or local fire trucks on stand by. But at Belknap Recreation Area, the fires were handled by the staff on hand up to 1963. (Courtesy of Laconia Historical Society.)

This photograph, taken by Aldrich Photography, is an aerial view of the Belknap Recreation Area. This picture shows the start of the 100-Mile National Championship Road Race. The right side of the photograph is the main campground. The campground was usually sold out during the AMA-sanctioned gypsy tour. The year 1963 was the last year that the campground was open during the rally until 1992. At the top left are the motorcycles that rode in the parade from downtown Laconia. In the center left is the base of the 70-meter ski jump where the hill climbs were held. The hairpin turn of the course can be seen just up to the right of the parking area in front of the ski jump. The course for the racers can be seen going through the trees on the lower right. The course then came back through the woods to the left side of the main campground. The main lodge is out of the area shown on the photograph. (Courtesy of Butch Baer.)

The Fritzie Baer Sportsman Trophy is awarded to the racer who does the fastest lap on a lightweight motorcycle. The trophy was sponsored by both the Berliner Motorcycle Company of New Jersey and Ducati-Messanica of Bologna, Italy. Joe Berliner stands behind the rider. Today there is a Fritzie Baer award presented by the United States Classic Racing Association. (Courtesy of Butch Baer.)

This is the ground-level view from the 70-meter ski jump, which is to the side of the racing course at Belknap Recreation Area. The Lodge Sparkplug Company sponsored rider Dick Klamfoth and many others. Many of the spectators found good vantage points that they could view the racers from. These vantage points included vehicle roofs, the roofs of any nearby building, and even the tops of trees. (Courtesy of Butch Baer.)

During the races in 1960, these Laconia natives, including, from left to right, Jim Macquarrie, Dick Muzzy, and Pat Muzzy, are at their favorite seats on "dead man's curve" at Belknap Recreation Area. Motorcycle week gave the local motorcycle riders a chance to showcase their state to riders from all over the world. For many, this was and is an exciting time of the year. (Courtesy of Pat Muzzy.)

The news media was always looking for a chance to get great footage at Laconia. In 1962, the Columbia Broadcasting Service (CBS) did a documentary on Laconia, which included the gypsy tour and the national championship races at Belknap Recreation Area. This documentary was done for CBS's Summer Sports Spectacular show, which was shown across the country and throughout Europe. In this photograph by Loran Percy, rider Carroll Resweiber is interviewed for the show. (Courtesy of Butch Baer.)

This group of riders tears along the course in the 1960 novice race on Saturday during Laconia Motorcycle Week at Belknap Recreation Area. The novice race had a cash purse of $1,000. The 50-mile amateur road race was held after time trials on Sunday. The cash purse for the amateur race was $2,265. The grand purse for the 100-Mile National Championship Road Race was $6,350. (Courtesy of Butch Baer.)

Seen here in 1961, Laconia mayor Ollie Huot is about to cut the ribbon to begin the races at Belknap Recreation Area. Huot really enjoyed motorcycle week and was a big supporter of the rally. The women helping to hold the ribbon were from the Motor Maids, a national motorcycle club for women with chapters all over the country. The Motor Maids held their national convention in Laconia that year. Dot Robinson, a president of the club for a number of years, is on the far left. (Courtesy of Butch Baer.)

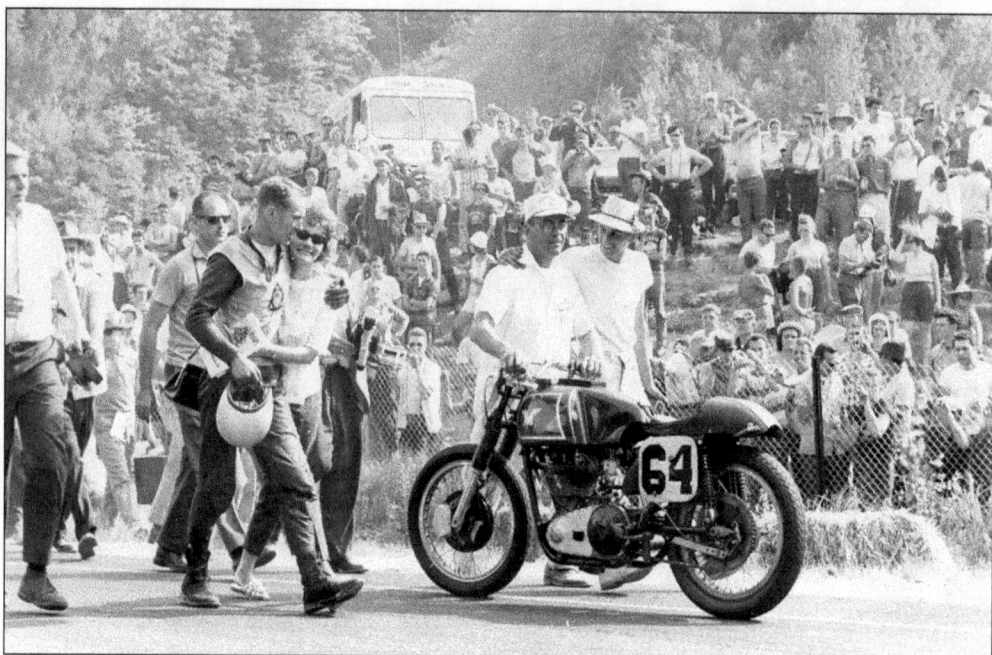

Dick Mann walks towards the winner's circle in this 1962 Loran Percy photograph. Al Knapp, one of Mann's crew, pushes Mann's bike ahead of them. On the hill behind them sits one of the mobile studios used by a radio station for live broadcasts. A lot of the fans stay on to watch the awards given out to the winners. (Courtesy of Butch Baer.)

Larry Martin, winner of the 50-mile race at Laconia, sits on his motorcycle between Walter Davidson of Harley-Davidson Motor Company and Al Wilcox, who is on the right. Harley-Davidson used the Laconia racing results in much of their national advertising. Their presence at Laconia was very strong from the late 1940s through today. (Courtesy of Butch Baer.)

In this 1962 photograph, the last 100-Mile National Championship Road Race is over, with the fans now making their way to their motorcycles or four-wheeled vehicles. The two riders on the left are carrying some exhaust pipes, which they may have picked up from one of the pit crews or from a dealer representative. There were no swap meets held at Belknap Recreation Area at this time during motorcycle week. (Courtesy of Butch Baer.)

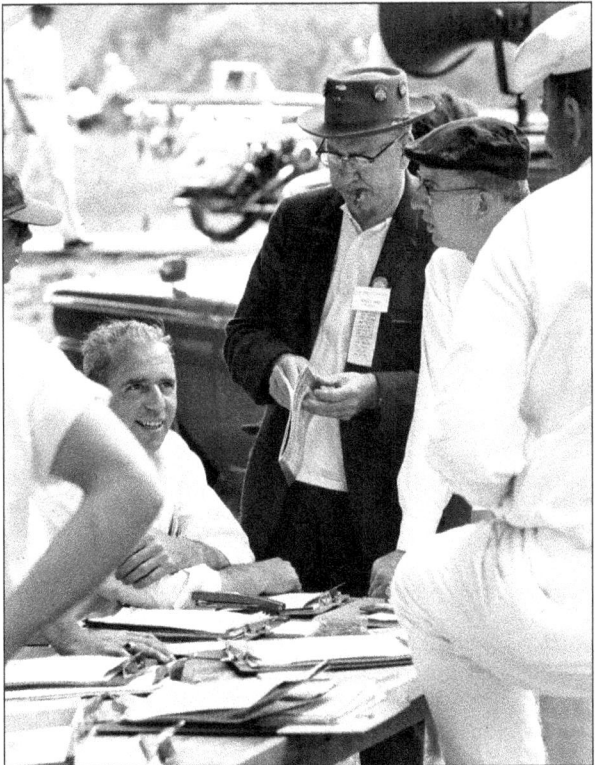

The title of this photograph could be "an official's work is never done." Fritzie Baer stands in the middle and is checking out the official program in 1963 at the officials' table, which is covered in clipboards. There were officials to deal with the many motorcycle contests, racers, flaggers, time keepers, and referees. The AMA also had its staff at Laconia. (Courtesy of Butch Baer.)

This Willard W. Wolfe photograph shows 100-Mile National Championship Road Race winner Jody Nichols (second from right) holding the trophy in 1963. To the right is Trudy Schietinger. At the far left is Ollie Huot, the mayor of the city of Laconia. Second from the left is Hank Westra. Nichols won the last race that was held at the Belknap Recreation Area until the 1990s. He had won the amateur race in 1962. (Courtesy of Butch Baer.)

This photograph by Loran Percy of Laconia was one of the last taken of Fritzie Baer in the winner's circle at Belknap Recreation Area. To the left is the 100-Mile National Championship Road Race winner Jody Nichols, No. 58, and to the right is second-place winner No. 94, George Roeder. Baer and many others did not want the races leave Belknap, but they were glad to have a new home for the races to go to—Bryar Motor Sports Park. It was the end of an era, with a new one to begin. (Courtesy of Butch Baer.)

Three

THE MODERN ERA

The 1960s are known as a turbulent time in American history affecting all walks of life. The motorcycle community was not spared from the upheaval of this time. The media made movies about motorcycle clubs and took aim at making motorcyclists in general look like lower-class citizens.

When Belknap Recreation Area cancelled all events and closed the campground in 1963, a lot of motorcyclists took this as a personal affront that they were not welcomed. In 1964, the AMA gypsy tour was held and included some motorcycle contests, but overall there was not much for the visiting motorcyclists to do except to hang out at Weirs Beach.

The so-called riot at Weirs Beach happened in 1965. By the time the Associated Press picked up the story and sent it over the wires, many thought half the city of Laconia had been destroyed.

Motorcycle Weekend was born in 1966, since all events except the races were canceled. One day of events meant the crowds from around the country were no longer coming. Fritzie Baer and others like Keith Bryar kept the rally going with a lot of effort.

In 1991, the Laconia Motorcycle Week Association was formed by area businesses and organizations. The role of the not-for-profit association was to promote motorcycle week and bring back visitors from around the world to partake in events happening all over the state of New Hampshire.

As early as 1963, Keith Bryar had begun plans to build a motor sports park at his location on State Highway 106 in Loudon, which is 15 miles south of Laconia. The name of the facility was the 106 Midway Speedway and it had a half-mile clay track. Stock cars and go-karts made up the action on the track. Fritzie Baer, the New England Motorcycle Dealers Association, the AMA, and others had encouraged Bryar to build a new track that could host the championship motorcycle races and other big-road events. Seen here from left to right are Bill Schietinger of the New England Motorcycle Dealers Association, Fritzie Baer, Bob Finn, and Keith Bryar. The Bahre family bought the track, now New Hampshire International Speedway, from Bryar in 1988. (Courtesy of Butch Baer.)

This 1969 Viking aerial photograph shows an expanded Bryar Motor Sports Park. The grandstand is just left of the small circle to the right. The track today holds over 100,000 seats and hosts two NASCAR races. While the track is loved by fans, many miss the days of watching the races while standing off to the side of the race course at Belknap Recreation Area, which is now called Gunstock Mountain Resort. (Courtesy of Laconia Historical Society.)

The mayor of Laconia, Peter Lessard, is seen in this Loran Percy photograph holding onto a ribbon with Bill Schietinger of the New England Motorcycle Dealers. Schietinger holds the ribbon on the right. Fritzie Baer is at the far right wearing his red hat. The start of Laconia Motorcycle Week in 1965 is being celebrated with a ribbon-cutting ceremony outside Carignan's Garage on Union Avenue. None of the participants knew that this would be the last official start of Laconia Motorcycle Week until 1991. (Courtesy of Butch Baer.)

The winner of the Laconia Classic 100-Mile National Championship Road Race at Bryar Motor Sports Park, Ralph White, No. 15, holds the first-place trophy. Jody Nicholas is No. 58 and No. 2 is Dick Mann. The Laconia Classic at Loudon began in 1965. Keith Bryar changed the name of the race to the Loudon Classic by the 1980s. This was due to his unhappiness with the way that he felt the motorcyclists were being treated by some city of Laconia officials. (Courtesy of Butch Baer.)

This Willard Wolfe photograph shows the winner of the 1970 Laconia Classic 75-mile race, No. 10, Gary Fisher. His father, Ed, holds the winners trophy next to Gary's mother. Fritzie Baer stands directly behind them wearing his red hat. By 1970, many fans were camping along both sides of State Highway 106 between Belmont and Concord. (Courtesy of Butch Baer.)

By the time this 1978 photograph was taken, many fans were camping on the land around the track at Bryar Motor Sports Park. Camping had been banned along State Highway 106. The Laconia Classic was cancelled in 1975 because of unrest along the highway in 1974. So in 1976, Bryar opened up all the land he owned around the track to camping. Tires have replaced bales of hay on this turn. (Courtesy of Bill and Sue Vachon.)

The front of the pack begins to lean into one of the curves during the Laconia Classic on motorcycle weekend. In the background are some of the many vehicles of those camping at the track. By 1980, as many as 10,000 people camped around the track. A canopy of smoke could be seen from a mile around because of the many campfires. (Courtesy of Bill and Sue Vachon.)

This group of racers is lined up for time trials at Bryar Motor Sports Park for the Laconia Classic in 1980. The stands are full on Sunday morning for the trials. The Laconia Classic 1980 banner is on the wall at the top of the photograph. There are no Harley-Davidsons or Indian motorcycles in this photograph. (Courtesy of the Laconia Historical Society.)

By 1980, many of the racers were not racing full-time on the AMA circuit. California racer Skip Aksland gets ready for the Laconia Classic in 1980. Gary Nixon won four national races in 1967, 1970, 1973, and 1974. Steve Baker won in 1976. Both Baker and Jay Springsteen were popular racers at this time. (Courtesy of Laconia Historical Society.)

Keith Bryar spared no expense at providing entertainment for the fans at the Bryar Motor Sports Park. Here Doug Domokos, known as the "Wheelie King," shows his skills doing a wheelie while riding over a car. For many, there were all kinds of different entertainment going on in other parts of the track, including large camp fires that lit up the sky. (Courtesy of the Laconia Historical Society.)

When the Bahre family bought the track in 1988, they changed the name of it to the New Hampshire International Speedway (NHIS). They also provided different types of entertainment for the fans. Here Doug Danger from Auburn, Massachusetts, jumps more than 150 feet over 25 cars. This was done during an accuracy jump-off against Dar Davies of Sidney, Australia. Danger won the jump-off competition coming as close as one foot from the landing mark. (Courtesy of Laconia Historical Society.)

Miguel Duhamel

Racer Miguel Duhamel was part of the Smokin' Joe's racing team and this photograph was used for their public relations. Camel cigarettes of the R. J. Reynolds Tobacco Company became a big part of the AMA grand national series by becoming a sponsor. So much so, in fact, that the whole racing program was renamed the Camel Pro Series in 1975. The races in Loudon were cancelled in 1975 due to the AMA refusing to sanction the event there. (Courtesy of Laconia Historical Society.)

This Boyd Reynolds photograph shows, from left to right, Ray Patenaude, Bill Schietinger, Fritzie Baer (on the scooter), Berkley Boren, Link Kuchley, Keith Bryar, and Tom Clark. They are talking just prior to the start of the race at Bryar Motor Sports Park. Baer stayed involved with the championship races, the Laconia Classic, and then motorcycle weekend until he passed away on September 7, 1984. Baer spent most of his life dealing with Indian motorcycles and motorcycle races during the New England gypsy tour. To Baer, it was his life's passion along with his beloved family. (Courtesy of Butch Baer.)

The grandstands at the Bryar Motor Sports Park are full at the start of this race during the Laconia Classic. Skip Aksland, No. 27 from Mantica, California, and Dave Aldana, No. 10 from Santa Ana, California, are part of the many riders from the state of California in the Camel Pro Series. The pine trees behind the grandstands are now gone with the expansion of the track. (Courtesy of Laconia Historical Society.)

This view of the stands was taken from the top of the tower just above the stands. Keith Bryar held short-track races at night a few times but most night activity continued to be in the camping area. By 1990, all organized nighttime activity had ceased at the track. (Courtesy of Laconia Historical Society.)

Sidecar racing has been a part of motorcycle week since World War II. The rider in the sidecar is called the monkey. The weight of the sidecar rider used to help keep the motorcycle flat on the ground while going around curves. A great deal of skill is needed to keep the motorcycle from tipping over on the corners. (Courtesy of Laconia Historical Society.)

The racers are burning up the track at NHIS in this 1994 photograph. The look of the riders has changed completely from the early races at Laconia in the 1930s. It is almost impossible to see the faces of the riders, and the present-day track keeps a great distance between the racers and the fans. Several races, including vintage, sidecar, and superbike, continue today at NHIS during motorcycle week. (Courtesy of Laconia Historical Society.)

This aerial photograph shows Weirs Beach during motorcycle week on Thursday morning in 1997, 32 years after the following four photographs were taken. This Winnipesaukee Railroad ran what was, at the time, New Hampshire's only rail commuter service. The train from Lakeport can be seen at the top of the photograph. After 1998, boats were no longer allowed to beach on the shore. The boats lined up in the top left of the picture are entering the Weirs Channel. To the right of that is the Weirs Beach parking lot now run by the Weirs Action Committee with proceeds being put back into Weirs Beach. In the top right corner is the Weirs Beach Waterslide. (Courtesy of the Laconia Motorcycle Week Association.)

This 1965 photograph by Bob St. Louis is taken from the west side of Lakeside Avenue. Across the street is the boardwalk and Lake Winnipesauke. This photograph was taken just before the incident that many feel put an end to motorcycle week the way it was up to that point. In this scene, there are almost as many cars as there are motorcycles. Many of the people standing around watching are local residents who were not motorcyclists. (Courtesy of Laconia Historical Society.)

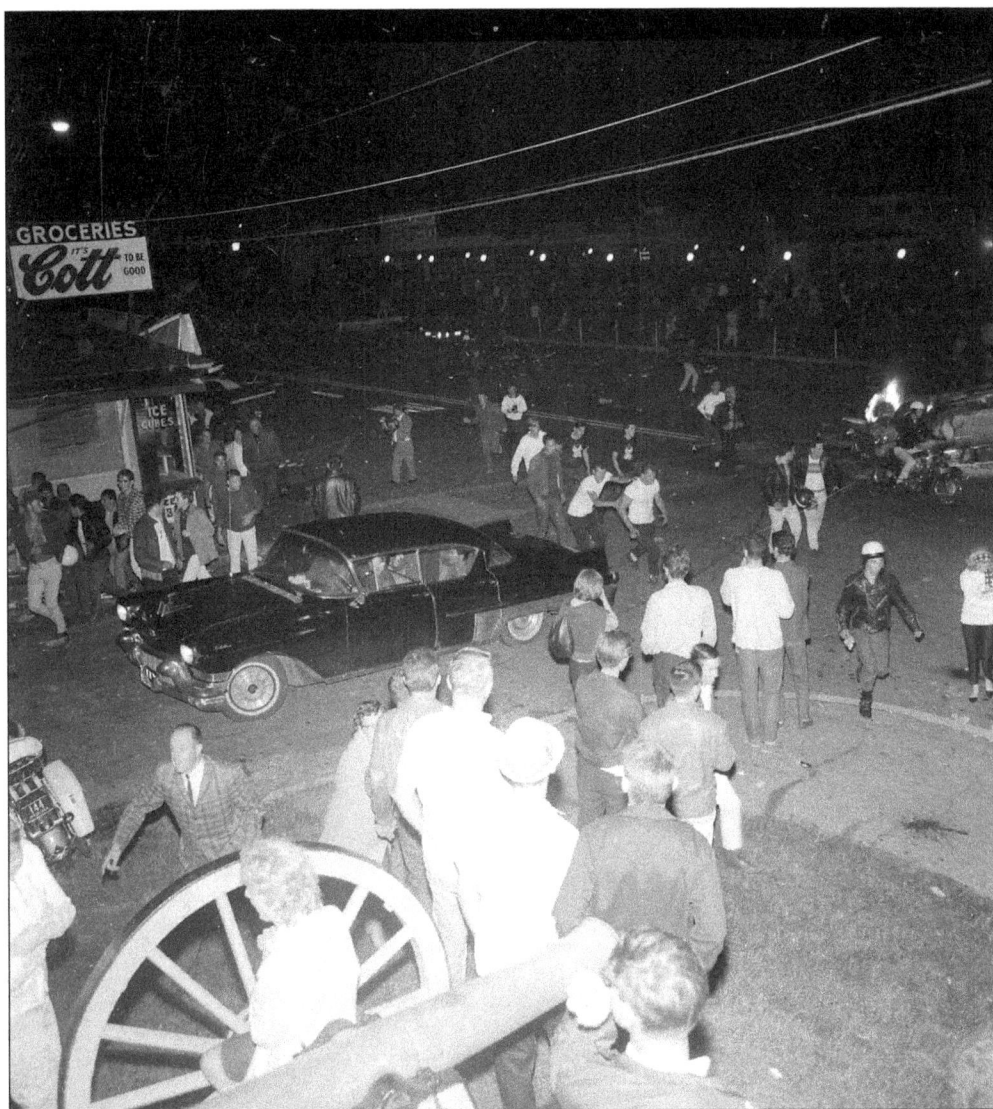

On the right side of this Bob St. Louis photograph is a fire just starting to burn. A car, which has been turned upside down, is on fire. The car, driven by a local resident, was reported to have bumped one or two motorcycles while driving through traffic on Lakeside Avenue. Some people have claimed that the Hells Angels Motorcycle Club was responsible for the trouble. However, there were no Hells Angels on the east coast in 1965 and there are no photographs showing any of the members there. Later the Laconia police chief told a news reporter that the "riot" had been planned by "outsiders" for over a year. The location of the fire was at the junction of New Hampshire Avenue and Lakeside Avenue. Most of the people seen here do not appear to be motorcyclists. Today the area in front of the cannons is covered with vendors during motorcycle week. (Courtesy of Laconia Historical Society.)

The crowd that has gathered to watch the car burn has grown in size in this Bob St. Louis photograph. The police had not yet begun to clear the crowd from the area. Also not in view is the New Hampshire National Guard, which had been called to duty for the rally and was stationed in the Laconia area in anticipation of any trouble. (Courtesy of Laconia Historical Society.)

This Bob St. Louis photograph has been seen around the world. The fire from the burning car lights up Lakeside Avenue in Weirs Beach. The police and national guard used tear gas, bird shots, buck shots, and batons to push the crowd out of the Weirs. The affair was over in less than an hour but, over the years, the stories have grown. Even today there are some who think that most of the Weirs was destroyed by fire. What was destroyed was motorcycle week. All events in Laconia were cancelled for the next year and the AMA did not sanction anything in New Hampshire in 1966. The mayor of Laconia, who had handed out awards that Saturday morning at the Weirs, later told motorcyclists they were not welcome the next year. (Courtesy of Laconia Historical Society.)

Because of 1965, many visiting motorcyclists decided to stay away from Weirs Beach except for a ride through. Many started camping along State Highway 106 between Belmont and Concord. This started in 1966. By 1974, the campers were packed in on both sides of the road for miles. There were heavy police patrols on the state highway and there were often incidents between the police and campers. There was also friction between two or three motorcycle clubs that attended motorcycle weekend in 1974. Because of this, New Hampshire banned camping along the highway and the AMA did not sanction the races in 1975. (Courtesy of Pam Paquette.)

In this photograph by Judith Rothemund, Joan Rohl stands by her Harley-Davidson Full Dresser motorcycle looking at her photographs at what is now the Weirs Beach Citgo Station. The bullet lights on Joan's motorcycle put on a colorful display at night. Judith took most of her black and white photographs, for which she is now famous for, either from the porch of Handy Landing or along Weirs Boulevard in Weirs Beach. (Courtesy of Judith Rothemund.)

Although many were camping along State Highway 106, the motels along Weirs Boulevard did great business during motorcycle weekend. But the police presence was very heavy in the area. Most intersections on U.S. Route 3 in Laconia had helmeted police watching the riders. This photograph shows riders heading towards Weirs Beach in 1978. (Courtesy of Pam Paquette.)

This traffic on Weirs Boulevard is heading toward Weirs Beach and is backed up towards Laconia. The police car is a very familiar sight here and all around the Laconia area. Tire marks show where someone has done a burnout in the road for the amusement of those watching traffic from the side of the road. By the end of the weekend, the road was covered with tire marks. (Courtesy of Pam Paquette.)

This rider has an extended front end on his motorcycle, which can create a problem parking on Lakeside Avenue in Weirs Beach. His exhaust pipes are also what are known as straight pipes, which may or may not be open from the engine, creating a loud noise. Loud noise is still a problem today and it generates complaints from many, and is the number one complaint around the country. (Courtesy of Pam Paquette.)

This trike, which is what a three-wheeled motorcycle is called, does a wheelie in traffic on Weirs Boulevard. This is all part of the performance for those stuck in traffic and those watching from the side of the road. With the lack of motorcycle events, except races and other shows at Bryar Motor Sports Park, visitors often had too much free time, causing many to produce their own entertainment. (Courtesy of Pam Paquette.)

This group of rally attendees is enjoying the sights on Weirs Boulevard. In the late 1960s and early 1970s, police would often not allow groups to enjoy themselves in such a manner. They were generally told to move along. One main reason why so many at that time chose to camp along State Highway 106 was because it was south of Laconia and they could escape many of these problems. Even though this group is off the highway, they might be told to disband and move along at anytime. Anyone who did not follow orders was subject to arrest. (Courtesy of Pam Paquette.)

This group of motorcyclists, made up of members of the Lakeside Sharks Motorcycle Club and friends, attends a wedding on the shore of Paugus Bay in the early 1980s. Weddings are still very popular during motorcycle week. They take place at many locations such as the photo tower on Lakeside Avenue, on Weirs Beach, rally headquarters, Gunstock, and other favorite scenic locations. (Courtesy of Laconia Motorcycle Week Association.)

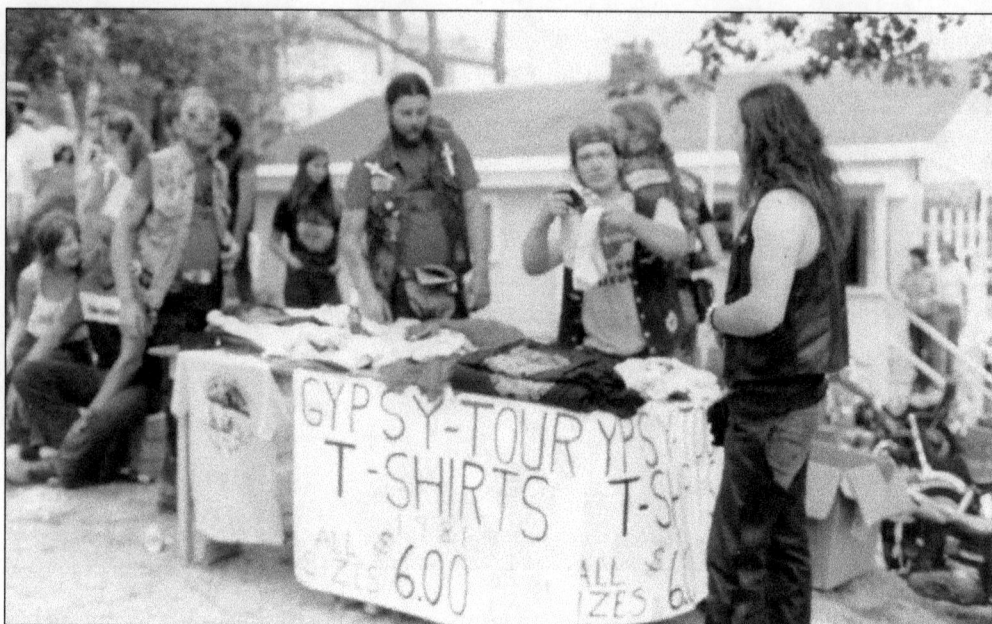

In 1981, the locally based Lakeside Sharks Motorcycle Club was selling its gypsy tour shirts on Weirs Boulevard. In 1981, t-shirts were already the biggest item being sold, but most were not being sold by local New England-based businesses. Today many t-shirt vendors attend the motorcycle rallies. There have been several Lakes Region–based motorcycle clubs since the 1930s. Most played an active role in the gypsy tour and motorcycle week. (Courtesy of Pam Paquette.)

This Harley-Davidson Full Dresser motorcycle is parked on the west side of Lakeside Avenue. The hill behind the side wall is used today by vendors who set up their tents and sell to the visitors and locals. In 1979, when this photograph was taken, motorcycles were no longer allowed to park on large parts of Lakeside Avenue. This was done so as to not allow too many motorcyclists in the Weirs Beach area at any given time. The parking meters were always enforced. This is no longer done during motorcycle week. (Courtesy of Pam Paquette.)

Here a member of the Laconia Lakeside Sharks Motorcycle Club and friend are heading towards Weirs Beach during motorcycle weekend in 1979 on a 1957 Harley-Davidson Panhead. By 1979, Daytona Beach, Florida, and its bike week had become the largest motorcycle rally in the United States. Daytona's bike week was nine days long and people from outside of the Northeast had stopped coming to Laconia because of the lack of activities and the unwelcomed feeling they got from some public officials. (Courtesy of Pam Paquette.)

This 1980 photograph shows U.S. Route 3 heading south towards Laconia. The famous Weirs Beach sign is on the left pointing down Lakeside Avenue. The *Chainsaw Massacre* is playing at the Weirs Beach Drive-in. The Weirs Beach Lobster Pound is beside the drive-in and the Weirs Beach Waterslide property is across the street. All three are major vending locations. (Courtesy of Raymond Reed.)

These rally fans are standing on the edge of the pavement along Weirs Boulevard watching passing traffic. This sort of gathering often brought an immediate response from the police, who would move the people off the right-of-way for safety reasons. The police stationed officers in areas where there was a problem. One of the spectators is holding a sign welcoming women to lift their shirts. Although this was common practice at many rallies around the country, it was not a welcomed practice by the majority. This went on until a city ordinance was passed prohibiting signs like this on public ways, much to the relief of many. (Courtesy of Pam Paquette.)

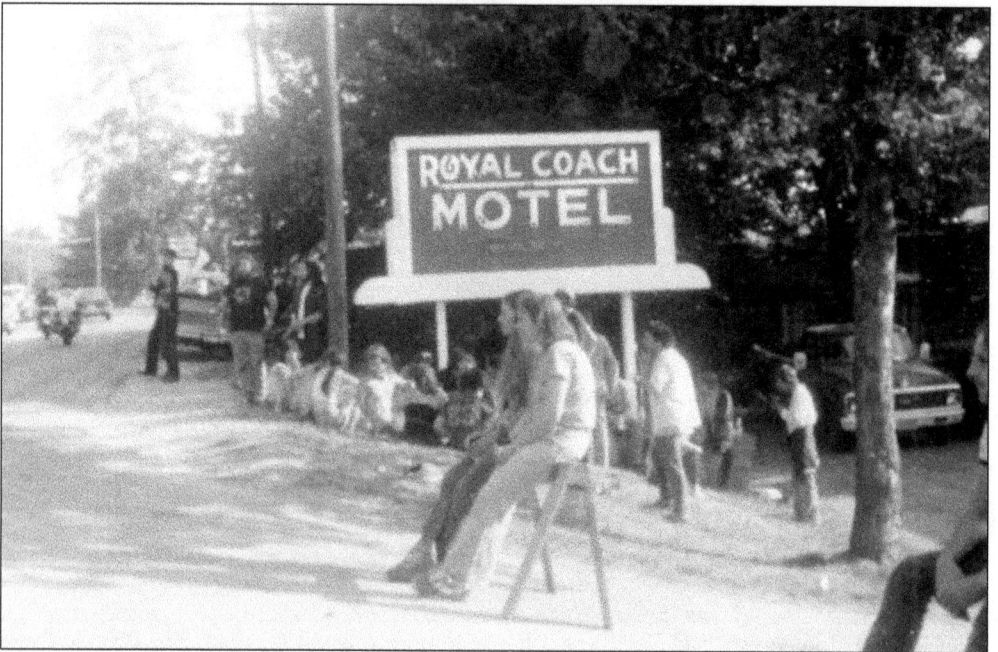

Here two police officers can be seen standing just off the pavement on the southbound side of Weirs Boulevard. Because of this, everyone else is standing or sitting back from the right-of-way. People-watching has become a major pastime for many who attend not only Laconia, but most of the major rallies. (Courtesy of Pam Paquette.)

This 1994 photograph from Laconia Motorcycle Week shows the front of the Naswa Resort on Weirs Boulevard. The owner, Peter Makris, was a longtime supporter of the rally. He had been a member of the Red Hat Brigade in the 1950s and early 1960s, and his family signed on early to help bring back a lot of the events that were part of motorcycle week pre-1966. The Naswa Resort was also a member of the board of directors for the Laconia Motorcycle Week Association, which was formed in 1992, and for several years helped to increase awareness about motorcycle week and the state of New Hampshire. (Courtesy of Allan Harrison.)

The parking lot outside the general store and Weirs Deli Mart on Weirs Boulevard is jammed during motorcycle week in 1994. Parking was at a premium during the rally. For most, if not all, of the businesses in the Weirs Beach area, motorcycle week is the busiest time of the year and has been since the 1930s. The general store today is Waldo Pepper's Pizza and Subs. (Courtesy of Allan Harrison.)

This photograph shows the staff and some of the riders at the first hill climb to take place at Gunstock Mountain Resort since 1962. Many are members are of the RidgeRunners Promotional Group that is in charge of organizing the hill climb hosted by Gunstock. Missing in the photograph is Sylvia Legget, who worked hard behind the scenes to get the hill climbs back to Gunstock. The first year saw 2,000 to 3,000 visitors watching the event. Today there often 10,000 to 12,000 people at Gunstock for the hill climb. (Courtesy of Cyclops.)

This photograph by Michael Frederic catches a young rider who is about to attempt the 70-meter hill at Gunstock Mountain Resort. With the return of the hill climbs there is no shortage of riders to make the attempt up the hill. The hill climbs are no longer scored on points, but there are trophies for winners. (Courtesy of Michael Frederic.)

In 1994, the Lakeside Sharks Motorcycle Club is selling the official AMA gypsy tour shirts on the porch of a house on Lakeside Avenue in Weirs Beach. The Lakeside Sharks Motorcycle Club had been on the board of the Laconia Motorcycle Week Association since its conception. The house in this photograph is now gone and is replaced with the Beachview Bazaar during motorcycle week. (Courtesy of Allan Harrison.)

By 1994, vending at Laconia had changed. The city of Laconia required that all vendors got a permit from the city for a monetary fee. Property owners had to receive site plan approvals for their area where vendors would be set up. The vendors in this photograph are set up on Lakeside Avenue, which had become wall-to-wall vendors. (Courtesy of Allan Harrison.)

This is the beginning of Lakeside Avenue. Traffic is made one-way going north during the rally and no cars are allowed on Lakeside Avenue from Monday through Sunday of the rally. Delivery vehicles can come through from 6:00 to 10:00 in the morning. This system has worked very well to ease the flow of traffic. However, it is also an inconvenience for residents who live on or off of Lakeside Avenue. Most have learned how to deal with it during the rally. (Courtesy of Raymond Reed.)

Karl's Restaurant, at the junction of U.S. Route 3 and State Highway 11B, was a very popular hangout during motorcycle week. By the mid-1990s, the restaurant was renamed Crossroads and some vendors set up in the parking lot. The area is now a vacant lot used only for parking and vending during motorcycle week. (Courtesy of Raymond Reed.)

110

Laconia mayor Edwin Chertock (left) is shown making a trophy presentation at Bryar Motor Sports Park. The mayors of the city of Laconia had been very supportive of motorcycle week since 1916. By 1938, a proclamation was given by the mayor welcoming the motorcyclists from around the world. This stopped after 1965 but continued again in the early 1980s. (Courtesy of Laconia Historical Society.)

Mayor Paul Fitzgerald and his wife, Cheryl, who are both avid riders, rest on the mayor's motorcycle on Lakeside Avenue. He was instrumental in getting the Laconia City Council on board to help with the growth of motorcycle week in 1992. While he was mayor, he also helped to convince others to join the Laconia Motorcycle Week Association to get the rally back to its original form. (Courtesy of Laconia Historical Society.)

For years, "Chief," a member and then president of the Naked Men Motorcycle Club, could be seen somewhere watching the action on Lakeside Avenue. Many others would stake out a place on Lakeside Avenue to watch the daily activities. While "Chief" was watching, he also became an attraction himself as many would take his picture. (Courtesy of Allan Harrison.)

Parking in 1981 on Lakeside Avenue was still restricted to limited areas because of what happened 1965. One such area is in the front of Tarlson's Arcade. The peaceful look of the gypsy tour, called motorcycle weekend in 1981, was about to change on this Saturday night. Tower Street is the street to the left of the photograph.

112

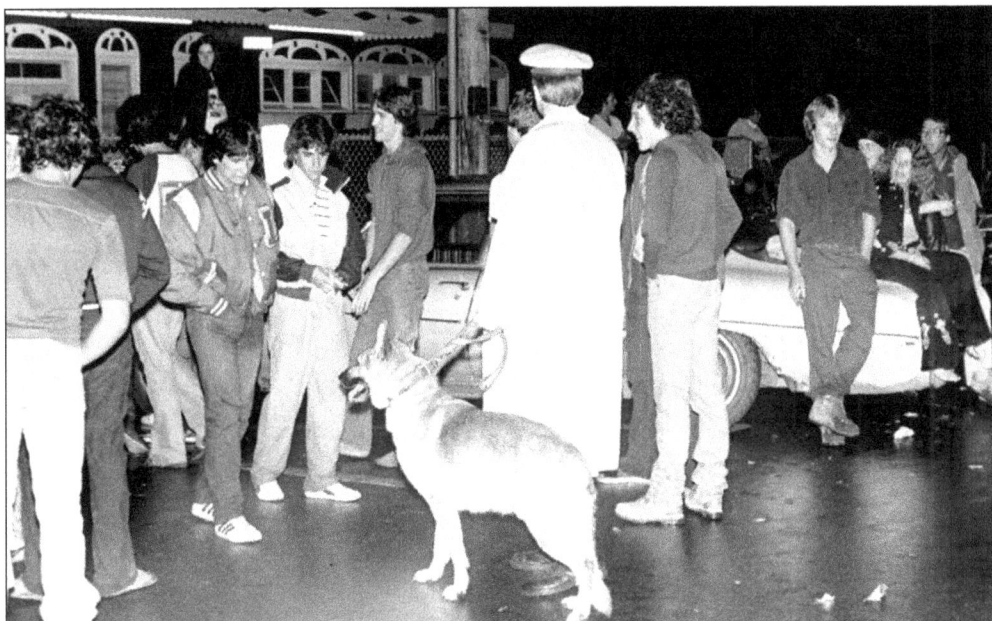

This police officer watches the crowd along the boardwalk in front of the offices of the M/S *Mount Washington*. To his right, some spectators are sitting on the back of their cars watching traffic. Cars are no longer allowed on Lakeside Avenue in order to free up room for motorcycles. No motorcyclists can be seen in this group of people. (Courtesy of the Laconia Motorcycle Week Association.)

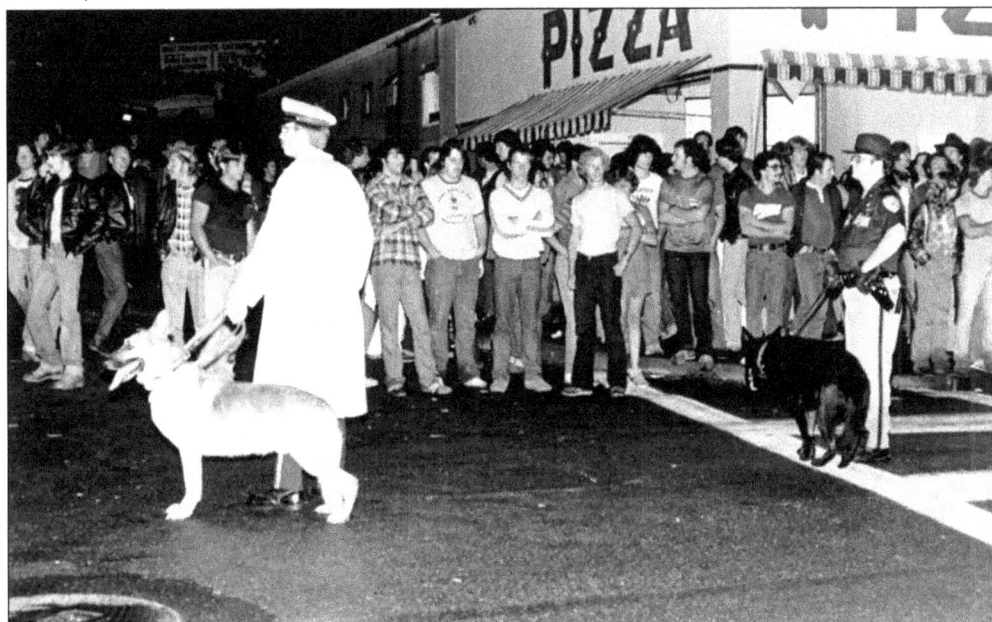

The two police officers and their dogs are being watched closely by a large group of spectators who are waiting for something to happen. By 11:00 p.m. on this Saturday night of motorcycle weekend in 1981, the Laconia chief of police decided it was time for the crowd to leave the Weirs and go home. A police line was formed across Lakeside Avenue and tear gas was then fired into the crowd. (Courtesy of the Laconia Motorcycle Week Association.)

In 1994 Laconia police officer Jeff Stiegler (left) and Hillsboro sheriff deputy Jim Hardy (right) strike a familiar pose standing in front of the Handy Landing Convenience Store on Weirs Boulevard. For many officers, motorcycle week means long hours and quite possibly extra income. (Courtesy of Allan Harrison.)

Laconia police officer Corey Fortson watches the traffic flow on U.S. Route 3 and on the sidewalk of the bridge over the Weirs Channel, which flows between Lake Winnipesaukee and Paugus Bay. The bridge is often a great place to take photographs of the lake. Some like to sit on the wall to watch the action but, for safety's sake, they are not allowed to do so. (Courtesy of Alan Harrison.)

Here New Hampshire state trooper David Parenteau walks along U.S. Route 3 in the Weirs Beach area. The state police have had a love-hate relationship with motorcycle week since the 1960s. Some do not like to work during the event, while others truly enjoy the assignment. From 1965 until the mid-1970s, many police wore or had their riot helmets close by. (Courtesy of Allan Harrison.)

This 1994 public relation photograph shows the New Hampshire State Police Motorcycle Squad by their motorcycles in front of Paugus Bay during Motorcycle Week. From left to right are trooper Darren Dustin, Cpl. Bruce Mathews, Cpl. Gerald Berry, Sgt. Thomas Wolkowski, trooper Steven Ford, trooper William Magee, Cpl. William Turner, and trooper Peter Gould. Their many duties included traffic control, public safety, and escorting parades and gypsy tours. They have done a great job with the parades and tours and the motorcyclists appreciate the effort. (Courtesy of New Hampshire State Police.)

Laconia motorcycle police officer Larry Fredette stands by his motorcycle in Weirs Beach. The Harley-Davidson dealership in Meredith gave the Laconia Police Department these police-special Harleys to use during the summer months. Now a lot of cities and towns have motorcycle officers. In recent years, the Laconia Police Department and Laconia Fire Department spend much of the year planning for motorcycle week. (Courtesy of Michael Frederic.)

This Indian motorcycle parked on Lakeside Avenue in 1994 is one of the many classic motorcycles that are parked on the avenue for people to admire. The plan for center-line parking on Lakeside Avenue began in 1993 and is an important part of the traffic plan. The photograph tower sits on the far end of the street in this picture. (Courtesy of Michael Lichter.)

In the 1980s, Harley-Davidson held demo rides at the Lakes Region Plaza during motorcycle week. The plaza, which is just over the town line in Gilford, was home to the demos until they moved to NHIS in the mid-1990s. In 2007, the Harley-Davidson demos and display were moved to downtown Laconia. Many of the motorcycle companies hold demo rides in Laconia and at other rallies around the country. (Courtesy of Raymond Reed.)

Two staff members of the Laconia Motorcycle Week Association get ready to launch the rally headquarters blimp during the rally in 1995. Rally headquarters had moved to the Lakes Region Plaza in 1994 and stayed there for two years before moving to the Weirs Beach Lobster Pound. It is now located at the Weirs Beach Waterslide. During the first two years of the association, rally headquarters was located at Funspot. (Courtesy of Michael Frederic.)

This is the walkway in front of the rally headquarters tent in Weirs Beach at the Lobster Pound. The Lobster Pound also hosted the Camel Roadhouse, a large entertainment tent that was sponsored in part by R. J. Reynolds Tobacco Company. The Lobster Pound is also on the board of directors for the Laconia Motorcycle Week Association with their neighbors, the Weirs Beach Waterslide. (Courtesy of Michael Frederic.)

Andrea Blais and her mother, Debbie Blais, stand in front of an official banner with many of the motorcycle week sponsor logos on it. Sponsorship has been an important part of motorcycle week since the 1930s. The rally headquarters tent serves as a place for people to register for the AMA gypsy tours and for rally information to be given out. (Courtesy of Michael Frederic.)

This photograph shows an AMA gypsy tour leaving the Lobster Pound on U.S. Route 3 north towards Meredith. These AMA gypsy tours go all around the state of New Hampshire to points of interest or for scenic rides. As many as 125 riders may take part. Unlike some rallies, there is no charge for these tours. (Courtesy of Michael Frederic.)

By the mid-1990s, Gunstock Mountain Resort had become as popular for camping and events as it was when it was called Belknap Recreation Area in the 1950s. Local tattoo artist "Rock 'n Roll" (left) of L. A. East Tattoo Studio is seen here saying goodbye to one of his friends. The photographer, Philippe Vermes, was from France, and he spent eight days in Laconia and then in Sturgis, South Dakota, for the Black Hills Rally doing a photograph study of both rallies. (Courtesy of Philippe Vermes.)

From 1966 to 1991, no motorcycles were allowed to park in front of the arcades here on Lakeside Avenue. Now the arcades are taken out during motorcycle week and the area is rented out to vendors. The site of the car fire in 1965 is just across from the pizza sign in the photograph. (Courtesy of Allan Harrison.)

This photograph by Deb Martin shows two riders racing in a flat-track race. This race, which came back to the rally in 1992, was first held in Cannan, then in Lempster, and is now held at the fairgrounds in Rochester. Beside flat-track races, other events such as motocross and slow races have been held around the state during the rally. Race promoter Pete Giammalvo of Sideways Promotions keeps working to provide the best entertainment for the visiting motorcyclists. (Courtesy of Pete Giammaluo.)

George "Lucky" Thibeault rode the Wall of Death Motorcycle Motor Dome from 1950 to 1994. His first year attending Laconia was in 1941. He loved putting on a show, and he always had a big smile on his face while walking around Belknap Recreation Area. He often said that making the ride to Laconia for the rally was one of the most important things he did every year. (Courtesy of Sparky Thibeault.)

Sandy and Norman Teff of the Lakeside Sharks Motorcycle Club get together during Laconia Motorcycle Week in 1982. The Lakeside Sharks Motorcycle Club worked with the AMA to bring back the national gypsy tour to Laconia in 1993. They remained the host motorcycle club for the AMA until they disbanded in 2004. The duties with the AMA are now handled by the Laconia Motorcycle Week Association. (Courtesy of Laconia Motorcycle Week Association.)

New Hampshire state senator Robert Fennelly of Dover presents an award to the president of the New Comers Motorcycle Club of New York City at Bryar's Motor Sports Park in Loudon in 1976. The trophy was for one of the many motorcycle contests held for both AMA and non-AMA clubs. After a brief lull in the late 1960s, motorcycle clubs were returning to Laconia in increasing numbers by the late 1970s. (Courtesy of Butch Baer.)

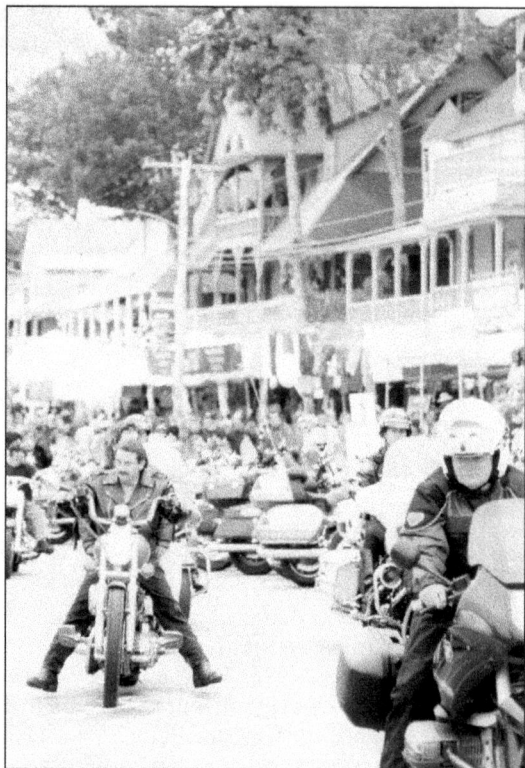

This view of Lakeside Avenue shows how congested traffic can get during Laconia Motorcycle Week. Riders have to watch out for each other because traffic stops suddenly as riders look for parking spots, and there are pedestrians everywhere. Before cars were banned from Lakeside Avenue in 1993 during the rally, traffic was even worse. The buildings that were built for Civil War veterans are seen behind the vendor tents. (Courtesy of Michael Frederic.)

This photograph shows a tightly packed Lakeside Avenue in 1994. The photograph tower, which in 1994 was run by the Laconia Parks and Recreation Department, is seen the center. Big John's Restaurant was a favorite hangout for visiting motorcyclists. The boardwalk is to the right side of the photograph. (Courtesy of Allan Harrison.)

The one-way traffic on Lakeside Avenue now starts on the first day of the motorcycle week as seen in this Michael Frederic photograph. For the locals and Weirs residents, it takes some getting used to once a year. Side roads out of the Weirs are blocked in an effort to have all traffic exit the Weirs out Scenic and Watson Roads. (Courtesy of Laconia Motorcycle Week Association.)

The POW-MIA Freedom Ride has grown to become one of the most popular rides that takes place during motorcycle week in Laconia. The ride was formed under the guidance of Robert Jones of Meredith, Jack Hayes, other members of the HD Riders Motorcycle Club, and Paul Lessard. The ride formed in what was the Lakes Region Plaza, now the Winnipesaukee Crossing, in Gilford. Every year, several hundred riders take the ride from the starting point and ride up Weirs Boulevard, down Lakeside Avenue, out Scenic Road to Watson Road, and north on U.S. Route 3 to Hesky Park in Meredith. Hesky Park is the site of the POW-MIA Northeast Network vigil. The parade is escorted by local and state police officers. (Courtesy of Daryl Carlson.)

For years, the history of motorcycle week has been stored for the ages in the work of both professional and amateur photographers. Some of those people are Loran Percy, Norman P. Speirs, Norman Brady, Williard W. Wolfe, Aldrich Photography, Peter Besh, W. E. Huntington, Morang Photography, Chet Brickett, Judith Rothemund, Dana Clarke, and Bob St. Louis. In more recent years, the photographers include Michael Lichter (seen here), Mark Langelo, Michael Frederic, Cyclops, Daryl Carlson, Alan MacRae, W. Stephen Loughlin, Bob Stegmaier, and Michey Halpin for filming. (Courtesy of Michael Frederic.)

The intersection of U.S. Route 3 and 11B at Weirs Beach was a very busy area in the 1980s and continues to be so today. The location of this photograph is in the parking lot of what is today's Donna Jean's Diner. Today, vendors set up in this parking lot as they did in the 1980s. Chet Brickett, a well known photographer in New Hampshire took this photograph. (Courtesy of Scott Brickett.)

By 1990, vendors were attending Laconia in larger numbers than ever before. The Sandbar Restaurant on the left is now the Weirs Beach Smokehouse. The Weirs Beach Drive-in had a large vendor area and the Weirs Beach Lobster Pound to its left also had a growing vending area. The Weirs Beach sign and Lakeside Avenue are on the right side of the photograph. (Courtesy of Raymond Reed.)

126

This photograph taken by Robin Sisson looks south on Lakeside Avenue from the second floor of the Weirs Beach General Store in 1995. The white photograph tower is left of center. The tower was built by students of the Huot Technical Center at Laconia High School. The proceeds of the tower go to the city of Laconia to help with the cost of hosting the rally. Motorcycles have to weave their way through waves of people while making their way north on Lakeside Avenue. The riders who came to Laconia and Weirs Beach for that first gypsy tour in 1916 would not recognize Lakeside Avenue today during the rally. Fritzie Baer would be pleased to see how relationships have evolved between the motorcyclists and the city of Laconia. Laconia Motorcycle Week means different things to many people, but for riders around the world, it is a big part of their lives. (Courtesy of Robin Sisson.)

Visit us at
arcadiapublishing.com

www.ingramcontent.com/pod-product-compliance
Lightning Source LLC
Chambersburg PA
CBHW050644110426
42813CB00007B/1908